The first million the hardest; an autobiography – Primary Source Edition

Samuel Crowther, Arthur B. Farquhar

THE FIRST MILLION
THE HARDEST

An Autobiography

THE FIRST MILLION
THE HARDEST

An Autobiography

BY
A. B. FARQUHAR

IN COLLABORATION WITH
SAMUEL CROWTHER

GARDEN CITY, NEW YORK, TORONTO
DOUBLEDAY, PAGE & COMPANY
1922

Ru

A773544

TO

MY BELOVED WIFE

WHO HAS EVER BEEN AN INSPIRATION
TO WELL DOING

THIS BOOK IS DEDICATED

PREFACE

THE eighty years of whose activities this volume contains my recollections show notable changes of scene. Beginning in a country neighbourhood, twelve miles from the nearest railroad; passing from farm to machine-shop, thence through the grades of apprentice, foreman, partner, and in time head of the business; attending numerous conventions; serving on commissions for state and nation; taking an active part in many societies and associations which had for their aim the promotion of the public weal; on frequent journeys throughout the country or abroad, making acquaintance with all sorts and conditions of men—my life, stretching as it has over that eventful period in our national history which began before the Civil War, has been most interesting to lead, and, I trust, may be found interesting to read. The assurance from many of my friends that a record of my experiences would be of interest, together with the solicitations of an editor that I contribute a series of articles to his magazine, finally overcame my doubts; and a stronger influence was the expressed belief of many that such a record might be of service.

However short I may have come of realizing my desire, my controlling aspiration has been to be of service, and if to the power to entertain, I might add the power to make my reader more zealous, more hopeful, more courageous in his own undertakings, I shall feel justified. Of this the reader must be the judge.

Too often when a life is closed our sense of loss is aggravated by the thought that so little is left to show the inner personality of the one whom we knew. The working of a man's mind and development of his character are interesting studies in themselves; and the increasing number of readers who appear to agree with good old Dr. Samuel Johnson's remark, "Sir, the biographical part of literature is what I love most," emboldens me to hope that this volume, whatever its shortcomings, may find a welcome.

The association with Mr. Samuel Crowther, in collaboration with whom these Memoirs have been prepared, has been most pleasant, and the friendship therefrom resulting I consider ample compensation for the labour they entailed. To him is due great credit for any merit the work may have. My secretary, Mr. Guy C. Stover, has also been of material assistance.

With gathering years one's circle widens, one comes into contact with more of his fellows, there is more in the retrospect, and I have always believed that in a normal life one should grow happier with added years. This has been my experience; and to those who read these words, I send greetings from the sunset trail, with the wish that they may find as much satisfaction as I have had in association with others, and that peace and happiness may attend them as they tread the road that now stretches far behind me.

A. B. F.

York, Pa.,
New Year's Day, 1922

CONTENTS

THE FIRST MILLION
THE HARDEST

An Autobiography

The First Million the Hardest

CHAPTER I

THE QUEST OF THE MILLION-DOLLAR SECRET

EVERYONE remembers the remark of the late Dr. William Osler that the initiative comes from men under forty and that older men might as well be chloroformed. Doctor Osler was one of my warm friends and he asked me to his home in Baltimore to dinner just before leaving for his chair at Oxford some years ago. He told me that he had gotten more reputation out of what he said in fun than out of anything he ever said in earnest—that he had jokingly advised chloroform for a lot of elderly college professors at an alumni dinner in an effort to jolly the younger men. And then I asked him if he thought I should retire—I was then approaching seventy. He answered:

"No, you have not yet reached forty. The years have nothing to do with it. It is one's mental and physical condition that makes age. You will probably be young as long as you live."

I have now behind me more than twice the fatal

forty years—on the calendar count; I have known most of the great figures of the nation during the last sixty years. I have seen the change from a farming to a manufacturing country, and have seen manufacturing grow from little-shop hand work to great-shop machine work. Many of the things that we use to-day and deem necessities were unknown to business when I first entered it. Other big figures have replaced the big figures of yesterday, but because, according to the formula, I have not yet reached forty, my interests are of to-day and of the men of to-day. And I hold that yesterday is important mainly as its experience becomes a mentor for to-day. If it were not for that I would drop yesterday and again be wholly as young as on that day long ago when I started to New York to ask A. T. Stewart, William B. Astor, James Gordon Bennett, and several other noted men the simple, direct question: "How can I make a million dollars?"

That journey, which—in a very literal way—marked my breaking into business life, happened in 1858 before I was twenty. The modern recipes for making a million dollars overnight and sold on a subscription basis had not as yet been invented. There were practically no books of business instruction; one just grew up, like Topsy, in business. But I happened across an issue of *Harper's Magazine* which described the successful men of New York, and immediately became fired with the notion that the way to get along in the world more rapidly than the next fellow was to find the secrets of those who had made the high scores. It was not that I was greedy for money, for the whole teaching of my father had been to the end that no one could properly be called a man who let his love for a dollar interfere with his love for a book— which is a precept that has always stayed with me.

But I did want to be successful in business, and yet, though success in business is not measured only in dollars, I then thought it was. Therefore, the question which I thought would most attract these several gentlemen and secure attention exquisitely compressed that particular philosophy of business life into: "How can I make a million dollars?" With that single query in mind I started fresh from my home in Sandy Spring, Maryland, to see the larger money kings of the nation on their thrones in New York.

I was only a raw country lad but had had the advantage of more than the usual amount of education, for my father and mother, although not at all wealthy, were exceptionally cultured people, and the family had been trained in the love of books and of study. I had never been to New York, I had seen little of what is known as life, and therefore it did not strike me as at all an extraordinary proceeding to talk to the country's rich men without the preliminary of an introduction. It never occurred to me that they would not be ready to see me or glad to answer my questions, for I had always been in contact with people who were glad to see any one who happened along and to answer their questions. Up to that time asking questions had been my foremost occupation. I do not ask so many now, but I still consider that asking questions is about the most useful way that a young man can put in his time—provided that he uses a reasonable amount of intelligence in framing the questions and digesting the answers.

That was a big, adventurous journey, and, by to-day's standards, a hard one, for the trains were slow, the stops frequent, and when one dozed off, the yell came to change cars. Of course there were no sleepers. It took, I think, fourteen hours of travelling before the ferry from Jersey landed me in what I thought was a very big city. It was then seven in the morning.

The New York of to-day would regard that big city as nothing but a fair-sized town. There were no great buildings; few of any kind had more than three stories. They were mostly of red brick and very plain and solid. Some of the streets were roughly paved but many were not much better than country roads and many were lined with trees. Above Canal Street it was country and Canal Street was a canal. I distinctly remember the boats on it. All of this I saw incidentally. I had started to

New York to ask questions, and the moment I got
off the ferry I went to the old Astor Hotel, left my
bag, and without waiting for breakfast started for
William B. Astor's office, reaching there about
eight o'clock.

He had two little rooms; in the outer was an old
round-shouldered clerk and in the back room,
writing at a plain board table, was a heavy-set
man with a full face and bushy brows whom I
instantly recognized from the picture in the magazine as Mr. Astor.   The furniture was unpolished,
there were no decorations of any kind, and a rough
mental inventory gave me a value of about $20.
The old clerk glared at me without welcome and
growled:

"What do you want?"

"I want to see Mr. Astor."

"You cannot see him.   He is busy," he growled
again, and then made a grab at my coat as I tried
to dive past him.   I shook him off and landed
somewhat ruffled before the desk of the richest
man in the country.   He had heard the scuffle and
looking up from his writing snapped:

"Well, boy, what do you want?"

I drew up a chair by him and said: "I want to
know how to make a million dollars."

Right away his testiness left him and he smiled
just a little as he answered ruefully:

"Do you want to make yourself as miserable as
I am, and stay up all day and half the night trying

to keep people from cheating you? I never made any money myself. It takes all my time to collect rents and to see that people do not get away without paying their rent."

Then he told me to sit down and he explained how his father had thought that New York would grow into a great city and had bought land cheaply in what he believed would be the march of the city; and then as time went on and streets were cut through it, he had sold off all but the corners, and these he had rented, and that he, the son, was collecting the rents. He spoke about the power of invested money and referred feelingly to what would have happened if old Moses, as he called him, had only put a penny out at interest and let it go on compounding.

"But," he went on, "there is nothing in it. I do not have enough fun. I am too afraid that people will cheat me and, in spite of everything, they do cheat me. If you really want to know how to make money you had better go to see some of the men who have made money and not waste time with men who do nothing but try to keep and increase what they have." I showed him the list of men whom I expected to meet, copied from a magazine. "Go over and see Stevens," said he, "at the Bank of Commerce, whom you have on your list; he may give you some good advice. See A. T. Stewart; he has made his own money. And then there is George S. Coe at the American Exchange

Bank: he is a nice fellow. And James Gordon Bennett has good ideas."

I thanked him, and as I left he asked me: "Do you expect to see all the men whose names you have on your list?"

I replied, "Yes, I shall tell them that Mr. Astor sent me."

"Don't do anything of the kind," he returned, snappishly.

"I am going to anyhow," I answered, my courage rising. "It is true, you did tell me to see them." He laughed a little and rejoined:

"All right, go ahead. You'll do."

Men went to their offices early in those days; they used all of the daylight. Shortly after nine o'clock I was at the office of John A. Stevens in the Bank of Commerce, which is now the National Bank of Commerce. Their four-story white marble building was almost the finest in the city and to me very imposing. It stood at the corner of Cedar and Nassau streets. To-day that is a busy point with the great Equitable Building hard by and more people passing in an hour than were then apparently in all New York. Across from the bank was an open square and above, at Liberty Street, was the Post Office with a steeple and looking more like a church than a public building. The bank was then an important one but it was only later during the Civil War that people found out how really big a man President Stevens was; he many times came to the rescue of the Government in the haphazard war financing. To my personal knowledge he responded to a call of President Lincoln and assisted in financing the first $50,000,000 loan.

I told an attendant that Mr. Astor had sent me over to see Mr. Stevens and at once he showed me in. Mr. Stevens had a somewhat better desk than Mr. Astor, but there was nothing of the modern bank president's furnishing about the place; it was all very plain and without the slightest thought that it was necessary to make a showing in dress or in furnishings in order to give an impression of financial stability. Mr. Astor had not been dressed any better than his clerk and Mr. Stevens might have been almost any one. In fact, of all the men I met that day only A. T. Stewart dressed and acted the part of the rich man. The others were decidedly below my estimate of how a rich man would be expected to dress and act. Since then offices have changed and many men, and especially bankers, find it advisable to surround themselves with the appearance of wealth, but I find that the really great men of the country rarely have ostentatious offices, and I know of none who go in for extravagance in dress. Now and then a man, when moving his office, decides that the new office will be something to make people sit up, and he hires a decorator, gets the finest imaginable furniture—and then hardly ever uses it. But to get back to

Mr. Stevens. He was very cordial and he laughed when I said:

"I just asked Mr. Astor how to make a million dollars. Then I showed him the list of people I had come to see, and he said you could give me some good advice."

"I am in the same boat with Astor," said Stevens. "I never made any money. All I do is take care of the money that other people make. The man for you to see is George S. Coe—and I shall send you right over to him. I think he has a board meeting this morning and if you get in there you will meet a number of men who can tell you more than I can."

With that he called a messenger and I was escorted around to the little building of the American Exchange Bank.

George S. Coe was, I believe, the youngest bank executive in New York, being then vice-president and afterwards president of the bank. He, too, seemed glad to see me—the Astor name had carried me along—and he asked me to stay until the board had met, when he would call me in. Fancy a metropolitan bank president of to-day holding a board together to talk with an unknown young man who desired to learn how to make a million dollars! But by that time I was quite at ease in the higher financial circles. Of the men I met at the bank I recall, besides Mr. Coe, only David Hoadley, Charles J. Stedman, William C. Langley,

and Edwin Thorne of the directorate—and Robert
S. Oakley the cashier.   They all talked with me.

The code of those men was extremely simple;
they were traders rather than manufacturers—for
New York had already taken on its character of a
clearing house for the overseas commerce, although
as compared with to-day only in a small way—and
the most striking recipe for success which they had
to offer, as I remember, was about this:

"Take care of your character, never break a
promise, and give value for what you get.   Avoid
speculation."   An old man whom I met in the
bank and who I think was Hamilton Fish, put the
advice this way:

"If you never break a promise, if you always
pay the money you owe exactly on the day it is due,
nobody will know but that you are worth a million.
And you will be just as good a risk as a man worth
a million, for all that he could do would be to pay
on the due date."

They had no short cuts to suggest and curiously
enough, not one of them even spoke of technical
or other proficiency.   They were concerned only
with fundamentals.   I gathered from them that
if one were scrupulously honest, industrious, and
economical, then the other business qualities came
almost as of course—but without the fundamentals
nothing else mattered.   In a word they confirmed in
me the lines that had been given to me in childhood
founded on the text that "God is not mocked"—

that is, that you cannot trifle with Nature's laws. And after all that is about the best recipe for success in business that exists. Having known many of the larger business men of the country during the last fifty years, I do not recall one who achieved any measure of permanent success who did not have these fundamental qualities. Men without them, indeed, have sprung up but their success has been ephemeral, and, although temperamentally some of these older men could not have managed the larger enterprises of to-day, the difference between them and to-day's successful men is only in what might be called detail.

Those men were elemental; they did not work through others as people do to-day. They did everything themselves. They did not have secretaries. They did not, as I later learned, delegate anything which required the exercise of discretion. They signed every cheque and in many cases personally made up their bank deposits because the handling of money was something which, it was considered, should not be entrusted to another. Stenographers or typewriters had not been heard of, no system of letter-press copying had even been invented. Even the busiest man wrote all his shorter notes by hand. The longer letters he dictated to a long-hand writer, and an active man could, without difficulty, dictate to two clerks at once. The clerk did not have to know a great deal, but he did have to be able to write, not merely legibly, but attractively.   A few of the big men had letterheads with their names and addresses printed on them, but the letters of the majority went out on plain sheets of ruled paper.   My impression is that William B. Astor did not have a printed, much less an engraved letterhead.   Since the labour of copying letters in full would have been very great, only the highly important letters were copied in full and memoranda of the contents of the lesser letters taken.   Sometimes the notes were kept in a book, but more often on loose sheets of paper, and, since there were no filing systems, locating correspondence and data was purely a matter of memory.

What made these men rich and powerful was not only their scrupulous honesty and high character but also, and this is a point I have never seen dwelt upon, their extraordinary memories.   There were no bookkeeping systems, the books were elaborately kept in so far as penmanship was concerned, but really all they showed was income and outgo. They showed nothing of costs and overhead expenses and the really big merchant had to keep all of his concerns right in his head.   A merchant had his business under his hat—no matter how great were his interests.   He knew what things cost, what they ought to cost, what they ought to sell for; he knew the accounts of all of his customers; he did not deal with strangers; he knew his bank balance from day to day, and his outstanding bills.

In fact, a great merchant kept in his head a good part of what it now requires a considerable book-keeping staff to collate, and it was the ability to do all of this and to judge character and estimate values as by intuition that distinguished the big man from the little man.

From the bank meeting I went over to see the founder of the New York *Herald,* James Gordon Bennett, at the office near the old Astor House on Broadway. Everybody at the bank meeting had told me that by all means I should see both Bennett and Stewart. I had no trouble seeing Mr. Bennett. He was in a little office all alone at a plain desk. I started to tell him what I wanted but before I had said a half dozen words and was just beginning to realize that his remarkably keen eyes were looking right through me, he broke in:

"Look here, young man, you look as though you had not eaten breakfast."

So interested had I been in my quest that it had not occurred to me to eat anything. Too many other affairs of importance had been happening to warrant bothering about breakfast.

"Whenever you see any one," he went on, "you ought to be at your best. You cannot be at your best if you are hungry. Go out and get your breakfast and then come back and we shall have a talk. Give this card to the head waiter at the Astor House."

I went across the street, presented the card to the head waiter who thereupon escorted me ceremoniously to a seat and served me himself—which, let me say, was a full-sized man's task, because the moment I was seated at the table I began to realize that I was just about as hungry as a boy can be. While I ate, the head waiter stood beside me and we talked about various men in New York, and especially about Mr. Bennett. When I had finished I asked for my bill and the waiter answered:

"There is nothing to pay. This is Mr. Bennett's treat. He frequently sends people over here."

Then I went back to the *Herald* office filled with a desire first of all to pay for my meal because I could not see any reason why any one should spend money on me. I started the subject with Mr. Bennett but instantly he dismissed it.

"Nonsense!" he said, "let's talk about something important. The really important thing for you to know as a young man is that you must bank up a health account. Look at me, I am never sick. I never take a vacation. I am here at the office early in the morning and sometimes late at night. But I always try to be in bed early enough to get a good night's sleep. If you get plenty of sleep and be careful of your diet you will never be sick."

And I think that advice is good. I have rarely been ill, I am in perfect health to-day, and although through many years I worked at least fifteen hours a day, I always managed to get six hours of sound sleep, and I still arrive at my office at seven in the morning. Franklin said that six hours is enough sleep for a man, seven for a woman, eight for a fool.

All the men I had seen until then had been glad to talk with me with the exception of Astor, and he had warmed up after the first few seconds; but they warned me that I might have trouble in seeing A. T. Stewart, who had a considerable reputation for austerity. I went to his establishment and was shown to the floor on which he had his office. Instead of being shut off in a little room by himself, Mr. Stewart had his desk behind a glass partition in the corner of a room of the lower floor, which was filled with clerks. He had established himself in a kind of observation post from which he could see what everyone was doing. I asked to be shown in to him but the attendant said that was impossible, that Mr. Stewart had either just started or was about to start home for dinner and could not be seen. He talked for a few minutes and after I had used the name of Mr. Astor we became quite friendly. He asked me if I would know Mr. Stewart when I saw him and I told him that I thought I could recognize him from his pictures. Then he suggested this plan:

"He will have finished his dinner and will come out of his house at exactly a quarter past one. He will have a newspaper in his hand and he will get on a bus. You get on the bus with him, get a seat beside him, and when he looks up from his newspaper, but not before, then you start to talk to him."

The plan worked, although I shivered as I watched him reading the paper, for he appeared to me a remarkably cold, stern, unapproachable looking man. I do not know exactly what I said to him at first, but he soon began to take an interest, and more especially when I told him what other prominent men had said of him. He talked rather generally on character and on always attending to your own affairs, and I went with him from the bus to his office.

As we were passing one of the aisles a man was sweeping up and Mr. Stewart's eye caught some rags among the litter. Rags were much more valuable then than to-day, because that was before wood pulp was used in paper making. Immediately he stopped, walked over to the sweeper and in imperious voice reprimanded him for his wastefulness. Then we went on into the office and at once I asked:

"Did it not use up more of your time to speak to that sweeping man than the rags were worth?"

"That's true," he answered, "but you will notice that I spoke so loudly that everyone in that room heard what I said. I meant that they should, so as to give them a lesson in saving, for money is made by saving—saving and investing. You get your profit out of the leaks that you stop."

He said that every penny which is saved ought

to be invested. The place to invest was in your own business, up to the point that you can there use the money profitably; that it was best to save so that whenever your business needed money you could provide it yourself and not have to borrow. I believe this is a principle which he scrupulously followed. I talked on various subjects with him and his assistant, Mr. Libby. I then asked Mr. Stewart if the report I had heard was true, that in selecting assistants or men for important places he gave preference to men who had been in business and failed. His reply was characteristic. He said:

"It is a great advantage for an employer to have men who have been in business for themselves and who have failed. The mere fact that they start in business shows that they have initiative and ambition, which are very valuable qualities. The fact that they fail on their own account shows them that they are not competent to manage their own affairs, and demonstrates to them that their best interest lies in casting their lot with those who know more about business than they do and who have the advantage of both skill and capital. This insures loyalty.

"Of course, these men must have failed honestly. I always look into the facts of the failures carefully and do not take a man whose business record is bad, but if his failure has simply been due to an inability to look after his own affairs and without any trace of sharp dealing, he is the best man for me."

A. T. Stewart was the absolute master of his business. As I have noted, all of the men I met were the heads of one-man concerns. Astor was the Astor estate; James Gordon Bennett was the *Herald.* They were despots, absolute rulers, and they were inclined to be paternal. It was unconscious paternalism that caused Mr. Bennett to give me a meal ticket. The most absolute and stern in demeanour was A. T. Stewart. All of them gave orders where the modern executive makes suggestions. And, although these men were elemental and meant to be kindly, they were, as I compare them with the men of similar calibre today, more arbitrary and in their business affairs more self-centred. They worked with things while the man of to-day works with people. They were in the way of being pioneers, and I suppose a pioneer gets pretty well calloused all over. They were busy because they had none of the modern facilities—although most of them were so jealous of their personal power that I doubt if any would have listened to the thought of delegating an essential task. I think, taken all in all, however much we may admire the characters and the granite firmness of these really big men, that the type of big man to-day is more interested in humanity and thinks considerably less of himself and more of those about him.

I cannot help comparing those men with Mr. Carnegie, although he, too, was supposed to belong to the old school. One day about twenty-five years ago we were talking about work. I told him of my practice of reaching the office at seven in the morning, and he remarked laughingly:

"You must be a lazy man if it takes you ten hours to do a day's work.

"What I do," he said, "is to get good men, and I never give them orders. My directions seldom go beyond suggestions. Here in the morning I get reports from them. Within an hour I have disposed of everything, sent out all of my suggestions, the day's work is done, and I am ready to go out and enjoy myself."

And that, I think, is about the most striking contrast between the men of yesterday and those of to-day—and on the mere matter of making money, Mr. Carnegie made more than all of the men I have mentioned put together. They were individualists—not managers.

CHAPTER II

THE EARLY DAYS IN MARYLAND

THE trip to New York marked a turning point in my life—the end of as healthy and as natural a childhood as any boy ever had. We lived in an old log house (afterward weather-boarded) with a barn that had been built some years before by one Ellis Pugh. It was called Cedar Lawn because of the abundant growth of cedars scattered through the grounds between house and gate, and our neighbourhood about the post office was known as Sandy Spring. We were in Montgomery County, Maryland, eighteen miles from Washington, and I remember very distinctly the great bonfires at the barbecues held at the end of the Harrison and Tyler campaign in 1840—although I was then but two years old. And I remember in the next year, when Harrison died, distinctly hearing the booming of the minute guns as they were fired in Washington.

Washington meant a great deal in our lives, even though it was only a sprawling village with mud roads for streets and a population of less than 15,000. My father went to see Harrison's inauguration and every little while during my boyhood I was taken there by him. Usually we took a trip on the steamboat which had begun to ply between Washington and Alexandria. I remember especially the great rocking beam as it swung up and down, driving the side wheels, and I thought it all very wonderful.

Sandy Spring, of which my father wrote the "Annals" in 1882, is in its way a remarkable little community. Its population was small then and is not large now. The people are mostly Quakers and descendants of the first settlers, and yet its plain, modest country savings bank has deposits now exceeding a million dollars. The prosperous "Mutual Fire Insurance Company of Montgomery County" has its principal office in Sandy Spring. The County General Hospital, built in large measure by Sandy Spring capital, is located a mile westward.

My father was a man of learning, having mastered Latin at twelve and Greek at thirteen or fourteen. He was unusually clever in mathematics, and was an expert in botany and other sciences. There seemed to be nothing in which he was not interested; like the old Roman, he had a part in everything human. Moncure Conway paid a high tribute to his "all-around education." He had never learned French, and came to Sandy Spring when he was about twenty. Margaret Briggs, who understood the language, undertook to teach him French while he taught her to play chess. The bargain was duly carried out, and naturally they fell in love and were married.

Then they went to Alexandria, Virginia, and my father taught school there for a year or two. Then he was engaged as a civil engineer on the railroad they were building between Baltimore and Philadelphia, the Delaware & Susquehanna Railroad, now a part of the Pennsylvania system. This lasted a year or two, and Mother meanwhile remained at "Fair Hill" with her little daughter Ellen, born about the time my father stopped teaching school.

I was born at Cedar Lawn, on the same site that is now occupied by my brother, half a mile from the old "Sharon" house, the home of my grandfather and great-grandfather, and still standing, having been put in repair by myself when I bought the old homestead. The central portion has substantially the same shape it had then. (There had been additions to the original house but they no longer remain.) The main entrance room is entirely unchanged, and I can remember as if it were yesterday my grandmother sitting there by the open fire in the Franklin stove. There were folding doors to cut off the draught from a portion of the room. The mantelpiece was made by my great-grandfather. At the time he built the house one could have walked from it to Canada without seeing a white settler. All was woodland and wild waste. His was one of the first houses built in the neighbourhood.

In those days swearing was considered a great sin. The Negroes were very religious and I never heard an oath among them. I never swore an oath in my life. I was but a little chap—six or seven years old—when these things were discussed, and I put swearing down as one of the things I would never do. Those things which I decided in my immature mind not to do I have not done. We were taught the sacredness of the relation of the sexes and the respect that is due to women. I remember an injunction my mother gave me when I went on to York. She told me never to forget the lessons taught at home but that God would often seem far off in the heavens, and I might forget His existence. But I should not be likely to forget her existence, and I should remember that she was with me all the time. "Don't do anything thee would be ashamed to do before me." I have always endeavoured to keep that rule. In fact, without being impressed by dogmatism, I believe in the essentials of religion and I have tried to live a perfectly moral life.

Another conclusion we reached was that one must give value for value received; that we have no right to anything in this world unless we give value for it. There are a thousand ways to give value. You can be agreeable and a comfort to your parents, and by being kind to them and never causing them any worry or trouble, you can repay them for what they lavished upon you before you were old enough to earn your way.

When we grew older each of us children had a daily task assigned. This was not usual in our section, where Negroes were expected to do all the work. We, however, were taught that work was honourable, and that by the sweat of our brow we must live. We were commanded to do our duty and earn what we could in some form or other. Ours were devoted parents, very fond of us children, and wishing us to have a good time, but during the vacations we had our several tasks in the morning and there were only the afternoons for play. Of course we enjoyed the vacations more than if we had been idle. I usually spent my afternoons in the shop provided for me in my father's barn, where there were a lathe and other tools.

Down in the woods we had a dam, and I remember that when eight or nine years old I made a boat. I was always tinkering with machinery or making something, and finally I could make wheelbarrows and other things used about the farm. I started experimenting with a threshing machine when about twelve years old, and worked on that threshing machine until I went to York, but I could never get it into practical shape. The anxiety to make a thresher that would work had a great deal to do with my eventually going to York as an apprentice in a shop that made threshers.

The people in Sandy Spring were very sociable. I have known a dozen to come to our house in their sleighs during the winter, or in buggies when the road was open, without any advance notice at all. Sometimes cook might be away and sometimes we had none—but they would come expecting to take supper. Half a dozen of the girls would go out in the kitchen and all in the greatest good humour cook the supper. The Maryland biscuit was usually a prominent feature of the supper. It was not long before the meal was ready, and after it they all pitched in again and cleared away the dishes; and they seemed to enjoy lending a hand.

Then we would have games, one of the chief of which was asking conundrums or giving questions to be solved. My mother had marvellous facility in answering any question that was asked, no matter what it was, more quickly than anybody else. While the others would all be sitting around pondering what was the answer, she would have a smile on her face, and was practically always able to give it. She had to be silent on many occasions in order to give the others a fair chance. We would gather chestnuts and roast them in the open fire, and have them for refreshments. Often there was a quilting party. Everyone was expected to have a number of quilts, and they were made of all sorts of patches and odds and ends of dress material, the women and girls of the neighbourhood gathering to sew them together.

My uncle, Isaac Briggs, was an athlete and very fond of nature and of walks—and I recollect as a little boy hearing him describe trips he had taken to the "Far West" which in those days meant as far as Indiana or Illinois. He said that on one of these trips he came to a little cabin where he stopped for the night, as was the custom in those days, since there were no hotels. He was welcomed, given his supper, and put to bed in a garret room. He always carried a flintlock pistol, which he kept under his pillow at night to protect himself. That was a lonely cabin and during the night he was awakened by the door stealthily opening; then a man crept in. He held a big, shining knife. My uncle could see him by the moonlight through the window and silently reached for his pistol and made ready. The man stepped up to the bed, raised the knife and—just as my uncle was about to fire he reached up to cut down a piece of dried meat which was hanging from the rafters overhead! After that, the horror of having been so near killing a man made him resolve never again to carry a firearm.

Uncle Isaac was full of stories, and ever ready to tell me his adventures. I once asked: "Uncle Isaac, what do you do when you get tired?" He said:

"Sonny, when I get tired on the road I just pick up a big rock and put it on my shoulder and carry it a piece, and when I throw it off, then I feel rested again."

He knew snakes, which were poisonous and which were not, and often had a snake or two with him. He had learned that there are very few poisonous snakes. He came into a quilting party one night with his hat (he always wore a high hat) on his head and full of snakes, and placed it with the brim down in the centre of the quilt. Then the snakes began to crawl out over the quilt, frightening the women but amusing him mightily.

Life in those days, looking back, seems to have been entirely free from friction or anything to make one unhappy. We lived so simply. There were no moving pictures, no shows, and no amusements, as we know them to-day. We took great delight in simple games, we had simple clothes. A box of candy was considered a magnificent thing. We always had doughnuts for Christmas breakfast up to the time I left home—they became so inseparably associated with Christmas in my mind that we used to have them for a good while after I came to York. It was only a few years ago that we stopped having doughnuts for Christmas breakfast, as a reminder of old times.

When I was about twelve years old my father, in connection with his sister, started a ladies' boarding school at Fair Hill, near Olney (formerly known as Mechanicsville), which became quite celebrated. He ran the farm too and made his family very comfortable, incurred no debts, and he left a substantial property when he died, of which I refused to accept any part, turning my share over to my mother and sister.

In our family, besides my sister Ellen, were my brothers Hallowell, Edward, Henry (first), Henry (second), and Allan. Henry first was a genius and Edward came nearly being a genius in "all-around knowledge," while Henry second, now living, is a mathematical expert. Once, when Edward was, as I remember, only seven or eight years old, we missed him for many hours and finally found him in the evening out in the woods. He had with him a copy of "Paradise Lost," which he had been busy memorizing. After a short time, perhaps a few weeks, he committed the whole of this poem to memory. He repeated it to us when we found time to listen. But the real genius of the family was the first Henry, who died before he was four years old. I was about eleven but he helped me with my lessons. He seemed to know things intuitively. My father and mother did not know that that boy could read at all until one evening when he was about two and a half years old, Richard Bentley, a friend of ours, came in and took the boy on his knee—he was a pretty boy and very bright and agreeable. Mr. Bentley had a book in his hand. Henry looked it over and said, "That is page 22." Mr. Bentley said, "How do you know it is 22?" Henry said, "It is two tens and two units." Then he commenced to read. Everyone was much surprised, except sister Ellen and myself. When our caller exclaimed:

"Why, William Henry," (my father's name) "this child can read," my father answered, "Oh, no, he has a wonderful memory, and he hears his brother and sister read and has picked it up from them." Sister and I said:

"Yes, he can," and we handed him the book and he read it right off.

No boy I have ever heard of showed more indications of real genius. He was unusually precocious, was very attractive, and had a queer way of every morning saying, "I will be brother Arthur's boy to-day," or "I will be sister Ellen's boy to-day," or Father's boy, or Mother's boy, and then attaching himself to that person with great devotion during the whole of the day. He was taken with scarlet fever, which was then a new malady, or at least rare, and was not at first recognized as dangerous. We did not send for the doctor at once. One of us asked him, "Well, Harry, whose boy will you be to-day?" He replied, "I believe I will be my Father in Heaven's boy to-day." He died that night. That was the first real grief I had. His death cast a lasting gloom over the whole household.

Edward was next to him and about three years older. Father stopped Edward's lessons and would not let him study at all until he was six years old. I remember that on Edward's sixth birthday he got up early in the morning and said:

"To-day I can study and can learn to read."

Father was unfortunately away that day and Edward was in a great state about it until Father came home in the evening, when Edward jumped on his lap and said:

"Thee promised I could read to-day." And before he went to bed he was hard at work at a book.

Our home atmosphere was distinctly intellectual. Father taught a class in French which used to come to our house, and several college students came to be coached in different studies. My brother Edward never went to college, but seemed to gain knowledge almost by absorption; he finally mastered thirteen languages including Sanscrit.

I never saw a drunken man in the neighbourhood. The Negroes seemed all to be happy and we had no slavery among the Quakers. There were but very few slaves within five miles of us, though we were in a slave state. Yet bitter as was the feeling against the Abolitionists, there seemed to be little and comparatively mild opposition to the Friends. The New York *Tribune* was forbidden by law to come into the State of Maryland, and the Postmaster told Father he could not have his *Tribune*. Father liked to read all sides; in those days of comparatively few newspapers he took many, including a French paper. He wanted the *Tribune* because he liked old Horace Greeley. He believed that the Constitution of the United States gave him the right to receive the paper, and that Maryland could not legally forbid his getting it. He went to Washington, saw the Postmaster General, and got an order that the *Tribune* should be delivered to him.

Father maintained that the Negroes should be taught to read, while it was still against the state law. In one instance a coloured minister in the neighbourhood was attacked for reading over the lines of the hymns to Negroes. A mob of people came across from the county seat, broke up the meeting, and drove him off. I was very indignant at this, and told the congregation to come up to my little shop in the barn and I would teach them, which a number of them did; and although the mob came up and surrounded the shop, I was not molested, owing to the great regard that everyone had for my father.

I was very much interested in ancient history, especially in the Greeks, and was particularly fond of Socrates and of Plato's "Republic," but Aristotle was then and is still my hero. As a youth I was a strong partisan of Hector, and was bitterly opposed to Achilles. I could hardly have been more than four years old when I decided that people who would admit a wooden horse as a matter of courtesy deserved to be better treated than were the people of Troy, that to accept the courtesy and fill the horse with soldiers with the object of destroying those who extended hospitality was a wicked thing. One of the earliest things I remember was my grandmother (who was very fond of poetry) repeating Pope's Homer's Iliad to me. She used to sing me to sleep with it. I would wander off by myself through the woods at four or five years old and study and think. I know I was not over five or six years old when I began to have spells of thinking that the world was a failure—there was so much unhappiness in it, and so much cruelty. It would break my heart to see a horse struck or a child teased or imposed upon, or any advantage taken of the helpless. I was much distressed because a cat was drowned by a neighbour for killing a favourite bird. I used to play with that cat and I did not think it was just to kill a creature that did not know any better. As I grow older those childish impressions come back, my love for the classical writings revives, and in feeling I renew my early boyhood.

My sister was smarter than I; she learned to read at five while I did not learn until I was nearly seven. We were taught at home until I was about eight or nine years old, and then went to a log schoolhouse about a mile off near the Sandy Spring Meeting House. That was the only school for miles around; some of the boys and girls walked five or six miles to and from school every day. We all took our lunches along and would play at recess when the weather was fine, and when raining and stormy we would sit around in the schoolhouse and repeat poetry and other things we had learned. The poetry I learned then I know still. Lochinvar who "came out of the West" was one of my favourites.

The evenings were often spent in reading aloud by one of the family. "David Copperfield" was read as it was published, and the numbers reached us, and "Jane Eyre" similarly. And we had Washington Irving besides. A good many other books were read which were rather abstruse for me, but my sister and the rest could understand them.

The memory of our happy home life seventy-five years ago is as fresh in my mind as though the events had happened yesterday. The habit of early rising has continued with me; I still usually wake up at half-past four.

Our home life was very happy. My father farmed, was a surveyor when a job offered, and also he delivered lectures around the country, but always he managed to get home evenings and then we would sit together around the open fire-place. Wood was cheap and plentiful and the fires were always roaring. He would tell us stories or we would read books aloud by candlelight. My father nearly always was the one who read aloud. Many times I have seen my mother mending stockings, rocking the cradle, with an open book before her. Afterward when Father began to be called off more and more, for lectures and one thing or another, and began to get home later at night, and we children had to go to bed at eight or nine o'clock, we adopted the plan of getting up at five o'clock in the morning and having an hour then in which we would all gather round the fire in the sitting room upstairs and have discussions or religious exercises—or moral (rather than religious) discussions. Morality was regarded as the basis of religion. Such questions would come up as: "Is it ever right to deceive or tell a falsehood?" I recollect one argument on this question which ran thus: "If you were sailing in a boat with a lot of people and a squall sprang up, and the only possible way to get safely to the other side was for everybody to sit quiet, would it be proper, if some of the people became scared and asked if there was any danger, to tell them there was no danger?" Father held this would not be a lie at all, for there would be no danger if only they all kept perfectly still. He took the stand that it was frequently proper and right not to tell the whole truth, but he could conceive of no case in which it was necessary to tell a downright lie. Questions like this used to be discussed in their moral bearings.

The thing that impressed me the most was the idea that God is not mocked, nor could we trifle with His Laws without suffering; and that we must suffer the proper penalty if ever we transgressed the laws of health, or morality, or whatever else had a bearing on our physical or moral life. This made a lasting impression upon me. I was of a philosophical turn of mind anyhow, and I concluded that if Nature exacted a penalty for broken laws, it was very important to learn what the laws were and how not to break them.

I remember having taken the side that a bad promise was better broken than kept, because if it was bad it ceased to be a promise. The lesson that I thus learned proved of advantage in a talk I had with President McKinley. He had promised two Senators the appointment of a certain official—the Minister to the Argentine, which position was then filled by W. I. Buchanan—a good man, but an appointee of Cleveland's—and although the proposed new appointee was not a fit man, the President insisted that he had made the promise and could not break it. I used the same argument with him that I used in winning my case as a boy of ten or twelve years old—that a bad promise is not a promise. Buchanan was retained, and my own friendship and respect for the President greatly increased.

The influence of those mornings, which were continued from my ninth year until I left home at eighteen, was of immense service. We always went over our lessons in the evening. With the regular school rudiments, we studied in addition French and German, and my three brothers had Latin. Latin and Greek never appealed to me so much because they were known as dead languages, and my practical mind revolted from taking up anything that was dead. I merely touched the Greek language, and gave but little attention to Latin.

My schooling in earnest, however, began at fifteen, when I went to the celebrated Alexandria Boarding School in charge of Benjamin Hallowell, who was well known in educational circles throughout the country. He gave the school a high reputation, and there were even some college graduates there who had frittered away their time at college and came back to learn something. Robert E. Lee was a pupil with my father in the earlier days, and his son with me thirty years after. Miss Mary Lee told me when I met her in Norfolk during the Jamestown Exposition, that her father had spoken of that school as having furnished the most important part of his education.

In school vacations I made a turning lathe because I loved mechanics. My father came to the shop and said, "My son, thy time is wasted in trying to do something thee cannot accomplish." But being a just man he called in a master mechanic of the neighbourhood, who said, "The boy is on the right track; let him go ahead," and I finished the lathe with his assistance, and it proved a success. I would always work at something constructive rather than play, though I liked town ball and chess. We took long walks in the woods, and studied the trees—learning to know them by the bark, the leaf, and the wood.

When I finished my course at Alexandria I took the management of my father's farm for a year, which served to renew my interest in agricultural machinery.

CHAPTER III

I WAS always interested in mechanics and had looked forward to becoming a manufacturer. I wanted to do something at once in a big way, but my father had too much common sense to permit anything of the kind. He told me that I could not start off full-blown but that I should have to learn a trade, learn all about the work from the worker's standpoint, before I could even think of directing anybody, and by the time I was through with that introduction to manufacturing we should be in a position to judge if I were fitted for manufacturing. I should say, in passing, that in those days there was more respect and reverence shown toward parents and older people than is the fashion to-day.

Having been regarded as a student and a lover of poetry and romance my acquaintances laughed at the notion that I could make a success as a mechanic. I was inclined to hitch my wagon to a star and my thought was to become a manufacturer in my own right. They thought I was merely going to be a machinist. My plans to them would have seemed like preparing for a trip to the moon.

My father having friends there, the most favourable place to begin appeared to be York. I went down to Laurel in the stage, took the train for Baltimore, where I was met by my uncle, John Elgar. A darky carried my trunk on his head down to the store of Anderson & Jessop, Mr. Edward Jessop being a friend of the family. From Baltimore I came to York on Friday evening, April 4, 1856, with Mr. Edward Jessop, whose daughter was later to become my wife. The first time I saw her was when we reached his home. They kindly took care of me at their home over Saturday and Sunday, when I got a boarding place at the house of a widow, Mrs. Alex. Immel, who charged me $2.50 a week, which included room, board, and washing. Mrs. Immel was very kind to me. I had a beautiful room, carpeted with Brussels carpet, a large wardrobe, and was very comfortably and nicely fixed.

On the morning of April 7th at 7 o'clock I entered the shop of W. W. Dingee & Co., manufacturers of agricultural implements, and was duly indentured as a machinist's apprentice, but with the provision that I might leave when I felt qualified to commence business for myself. It was my intention to learn the business in all its phases. It was a little place employing about ten workmen; we thought of it as rather a large shop. According to modern ideas it was not much of a shop although it was fairly well equipped with lathes, a planer,

and some woodworking machinery.   A man to be
a machinist then had to be able to do almost any
kind of metal work.   He had to know how to
chip and file to nearly the accuracy of a modern
planer.   The absolute mastery of the chisel and
the file was essential before a man could think of
calling himself a machinist.   We had lathes and
drill presses and forges, but only one small planer.
Adjustments were made by hand; there were no
automatic machines.   There were no turret lathes
to perform half a dozen operations without re-
adjustment.   Each operation was a separate en-
tity for which the mechanic had to select the
proper tool.

He not only had to select his tools and keep them
properly ground, but in most cases he had to make
them himself.   We had no designated tool makers;
every machinist was expected to know how to make
his own tools.   Indeed, as there were few first-
class tools to be had, most of the machinery we
needed we made there too, the shop buying the
raw material.   Practically everything entering
into the product, including bolts, etc., was made
on the premises.

It was the men's custom to play pranks on a
new apprentice.   He had to go through something
not unlike a college hazing.   After I had been there
a little while and had been subjected to the usual
run of fairly rough but good-natured fun, just as
I was leaving the shop one evening I saw one of

the workmen take off the brass plate containing a list of the special gearing of the lathe needed for cutting screws. He knew I had to cut a number of different threads the following morning. I saw that he wished to put me in a hole and make me call for help. Not wishing to be made a butt, I went down to the shop that night, calculated the gears necessary for the screws, marked them with chalk, and the next morning put them properly together without assistance from any one. That was considered by my fellow workmen as a feat approaching the marvellous, for they had never calculated the gears, but had placed them solely from the schedule on the brass plate and they thought that if once they took this plate off, no one could put them on again correctly unless he remembered the old order. They knew nothing of the mathematics of gears. I treated the matter indifferently as a matter of course. After that I was never bothered.

The employees became my warm friends. I think I managed to get the worker's point of view and that I have never lost it. We all called each other by our first names. In these days, and after I commenced business, I always knew my men by their given names, and none of the men in the early stages of my business so much as thought of "mistering" me. That was the custom in the old times and I think it would have been difficult for the old-time employer to persuade men to work for him if he had insisted upon any formality. Men belonged to the shop where they had started to work. Usually they had started their apprenticeship there and they continued to stay in that ship as long as it continued business. Labour turnover was almost negligible. When a man left his job everybody around wanted to know what was the matter. One afternoon a machinist came to us in high dudgeon from another shop and asked for a job. We wanted to know what was the matter, at once—why had he left his old place? We never "stole" employees.

"It was this way," he said. "The boss was out walking with a lady the other night and I passed him and said, 'How do you do, Harry?' and the next day he came around to me and said, 'When I am out walking with a lady in the evening I don't want you to speak to me.' I won't work for a man who acts that way."

The men were always interested in their work. It was a very usual thing for two or three workmen to start out in the evenings or on holidays to walk out in the country just to see how a machine they had made was working. For when a man made anything he considered it his own; he felt personally disgraced if it did not work well. A lot of the machinery we made in that shop was scattered around the country near York, and I venture to say that every man in the shop knew just how each machine was performing. Thus were the creative instinct and a genuine interest in the employer's business fostered—the desire to make a machine that would do the work for which it was designed, and do it well. Therefore, as a rule, the workmen could be depended upon to exercise their best judgment and skill on the work in hand.

As contrasted with the worker of to-day I think the older workman was happier because his wants were less, but there is no question in my mind but that he was materially not nearly so well off as is the man of to-day. The older man had more skill of hand. He depended on his own ingenuity rather than on the ingenuity of his tools. He worked by rule of thumb. When we laid out a machine we drafted to full size on a big wooden board and the men measured from that and not from a blue print. We had no blue prints, and I doubt if any of the men could have worked from scale. They had great skill of hand and eye, and, while their minds were actively employed upon the work in hand, there was comparatively slight emphasis put upon saving labour or speeding production. There was little planning ahead or thought of sequence of operations, and no idea of saving steps.

We kept out of one another's way more or less by habit, and although we worked hard from seven in the morning until six at night, a great deal of this time was wasted waiting for a turn to sharpen tools at a grindstone, or getting together to move some heavy piece of material, or hunting for needed tools or material, and naturally we got far less accomplished than to-day with improved tools and methods. The workers as a rule lived in comfortable little houses, but none of these houses had conveniences as we know them. The first bathroom with toilet accessories was introduced in a York house about sixty-four years ago, and people said a man who would put such things in his house lacked a sense of decency. Nearly every house had its own garden; the people were contented and managed to supply their modest wants.

The wage of a mechanic did not at that time in York average more than 90 cents to a dollar a day. George Reisinger was then looked up to as the highest-paid machinist in the factory in which I worked, or indeed in the town of York, and he got $1.12 a day. On this the men could live, for most things were very cheap, although tea, coffee, and sugar, termed luxuries then, were more expensive than they had been up to the time of the runaway prices of the great war. Wages were low, but people, as a rule, were very much more economical. What were regarded as luxuries then are looked upon as necessities now. Their wants were few and simple.

They had plenty of amusement but little of it cost anything. The church was the usual centre where they got their recreation, although, being in a country district, they frequently went off shooting or fishing—more often fishing than shooting, for firearms were expensive. A suit of clothes would serve a man, first, as his Sunday best, and next, as a working suit, for years. On week days they did not so much care how they looked and the ordinary working suit was not discarded until entirely worn out—until there were no places left on which to hang patches. In summer some of the men and practically all of the children went barefooted. A woman's best dress—and it was the care of every woman to have one best dress to be worn on special occasions only—was expected to do for years. Fashions were much less despotic than to-day. But really, clothing was not expensive. Nearly all women made their own dresses, and if they did not make them in the first place they were made by a local dressmaker and then made over every few years by the lady herself. I remember the wife of the richest man in York telling us one day when I remarked, "You look as if you had just jumped out of a bandbox," that every visible thing she had on cost less than $10. She, of course, made her clothing herself, including her hat.

When a man wanted a suit, first he bought the cloth, and then he hired a tailor to make it. Tailors made suits; they did not sell cloth. Just before I was married I bought some fine cloth and took it to Marcus Carroll, our fashionable tailor, to be made up. He felt it carefully and said:

"This is such a fine piece of goods I shall have to charge you a little extra for making it up. I usually charge about $2.00 for the buttons and the making; however, I think I ought to charge you about $2.75 for this, seeing that it is your wedding suit, but I shall split the difference and do it for $2.50, if that is all right."

I was married on the 26th of September, 1860, to Elizabeth N. Jessop, daughter of my father's friend, Edward Jessop. Since I have no words to express the blessing which the daily companionship of my wife has brought me, I will not attempt it. It is my great good fortune to have her with me still. Without her, life would be for me a barren waste.

Sixty years ago, after I was married, we paid $84 a year for a very comfortable house, a domestic servant could be had for $3 a month and board, a washer-woman charged but twenty-five cents a day, coming early in the morning and doing the ironing in the afternoon, while farm-hands were rarely paid more than $10 a month. When I travelled about the country, selling, the ordinary country hotel would charge me for a night's lodging, supper, breakfast, the feeding and stabling of my horse and buggy, the large sum of $1.50. A good hotel in Baltimore charged twenty-five cents a night for a room. Delmonico's in New

York was considered almost the ultimate in expense because they charged $2.50 a day for a room and meals on the American plan. The Astor charged $2 a day for the same service.

Our life was simple. We had very little—but we wanted very little. The average imagination did not go far. Only the exceptional workman ever expected to be an employer. In most cases he knew that, in the ordinary run of events, he would not have money enough to set up for himself, although goodness knows that did not take much money. Perhaps what held him back more than a lack of money was his fear of failure. The men were independent in the popular sense of not kow-towing to any one, but they were very dependent as far as money was concerned, and affairs were conducted on such a small scale that the possibility of even the employer acquiring a great fortune was considered remote. A man who was worth $20,000 or $25,000 in those days was considered quite well off. All sorts of expedients were used to save money. I remember one of the richest men in town—a book lover—used to order an occasional book in Baltimore and ask my father-in-law to bring it up with him when he came home Friday evenings, in order to save the expressage. Street cars would have been of no use in those days. Nobody would have ridden in them. It would have been too costly a pleasure—or convenience.

The employer dressed a little better than his workers and he had a little better house, and if he were successful he had some money in the bank, but the average employer had not a noticeably larger mental outlook than the employee and very few of them were forward-looking. Usually they thought that the way to do anything was the way it had been done before. They were very suspicious of new ideas.

I often hear to-day of radical and other speakers who, expounding the Marx doctrines that in the present organization of society the condition of the worker will constantly become lower and the condition of the employer constantly higher, speak of those older days as though they contained more than does to-day for the worker. That is entirely untrue. The growth of capital, the growth of labour-saving machinery, and the numerous aids to the power of a man's hand have, it is true, caused fortunes to be accumulated. Many rich men have been created, but all the wealth of the rich people is a negligible sum as compared with what these instruments of capital have done for the wealth of the worker in mass.

If the workman of to-day does not save it is his own fault. The expert machinist as he survives to-day frequently has a good house and he would scorn to live in the houses of the highest paid of the old machinists. He has conveniences which he regards as necessities that the older man never even thought of, much less acquired. He has books if he wants them, he has access to any amount of free education. His children have the advantages of free schools. Horace Mann and Thaddeus Stevens had not yet introduced the free-school system in the early days to which I have been referring. If his children have to support him in his old age, as a rule it is only because he has not been economical. Those children receive a better education than many of the children of the wealthy sixty years ago.

To-day as between the larger employer and the worker there is more distinction of wealth than there was in the earlier period. There is less shared interest in work. The employer is not nearly so close to his men and probably neither the employer nor the employee is as happy as he used to be. But that is because we all have more —not less; it is more difficult to satisfy the complex tastes of to-day than it was to satisfy the very simple ones of half a century or more ago. Happiness is said to be a freedom from want. We have all been educated to want more. Both the worker and the employer of to-day know of more things that they would like to have than did their elder brothers. As things go in this world, although we prefer to think of contentment as a virtue, the only people who approach contentment are those without ambition. The worker of to-day, however grievous he may think his wrongs, is far less of a slave to his job and to his employer than was the older workman.

An apprenticeship was expected to last through at least four years, but I worked especially hard during my first year and a half trying to master all of the business in the shop, and in the evenings I studied draughting and went at night to a business school in York which taught bookkeeping and writing. I entered as an apprentice with the view of later branching out for myself, and with the understanding that I was not bound to any length of time. At the end of eighteen months, and although I was but twenty years old, I thought I was ready to begin on my own account, and so informed my employers. By that time I was doing the draughting for the firm and also kept a record of all of the sizes and shapes.

Indeed, I was a general bureau of information, or factory expert, or whatever you might choose to call my nameless job. I introduced a little order into the chaos. We were only typical of the average shop; we had very little in the way of an office, kept practically no books excepting day book and cash book, had no inventory record, and never knew what anything cost. The prices were based on what other manufacturers were charging but entirely without regard to overhead or any charge other than that of material and direct labour, and these were known only in gross figures. I must really have made myself rather valuable in contributing order although that point had not occurred to me. The firm laughed at my notion that I might start in business, but asked me not to leave for a month. At the end of that month, when I was getting ready to leave, they offered me a partnership. I got in touch with my father and he thought it was safer for me to begin as a part-proprietor in a business that was already established rather than to start alone, and so he advanced the small sum of money necessary to buy an interest. In that he showed fine judgment; it is safer to take something that is going than to start afresh.

We arrived at the value of my interest by a rough appraisal of the business but without taking into account goodwill. When I brought up the matter of goodwill neither of the partners knew what I was talking about and I probably should not have known myself had I not made what I then thought a profound study of that subject in my business course. The fact was that a valuable asset of that business was goodwill, as compared with the simple machinery and small amount of stock carried.

Our trade was largely with the South, and very shortly after I entered the partnership I began to be a sales agent. Selling was not a separate division at the time. Whenever work slackened, one of the partners hitched his horse and buggy and started out for orders. I became a salesman

only because the older men did not like the idea
of being away from home.   Often I was away two
or three weeks, travelling with only my horse and
buggy.

It was difficult to reach some of the Southern
planters for they were high-and-mighty individuals
who spent much of their time hunting, and left
business to their factors or overseers.   One man
in particular to whom I wanted to sell agricultural
machines was the well-known Colonel Ned Lloyd,
who had a big estate on the eastern shore of
Maryland, near Easton, and who was the largest
slave-owner in Maryland.   He also owned a
plantation in Louisiana.   Fred Douglas, by the
way, had been one of his slaves.   As I could not
sell anything to the overseer, and it was difficult
to reach the Colonel himself, I was in something
of a quandary.   I was sure that if I could once
gain the house and form an acquaintance with
members of the family, the rest would be comparatively easy.   In those days Southern families
of prominence had darky major-domos who assumed to rule and were not inclined to welcome
any one who came on business.   Once having
gained admittance, however, the open and kindly
hospitality of the period would make you welcome.

An acquaintance told me it was important to
make an impression on the major-domo and meet
the family, when I should be almost certain to be
asked to stop over, and that after dinner I could

talk to the Colonel if he happened to be at home. He was seldom to be seen during the day, as he was nearly always out riding over his estate or hunting. I got the finest team I could in Easton, the county seat, and was driven down to Colonel Lloyd's in some state. On arriving at the house, an old and grave darky, who might be called the butler, received me. He spoke very deliberately and there was no doubt that he was a personage of considerable consequence. I handed him my card and under the card placed a dollar. He looked me over and, my appearance seeming to satisfy him, ushered me into the drawing room. In a little while Mrs. Lloyd, who was a delightful lady, came down; we had some music and talked about music and books in which we happened to be most interested, and after a while the Colonel himself came breezily in. I supposed it was growing near dinner and started to thank Mrs. Lloyd for the afternoon and said that I must go.

"You are too late," broke in the Colonel. "I have sent your team and buggy back to Easton. You are going to stay all night and to-morrow we shall look over the place."

We had a delightful evening. The next morning we rode around the estate. I pointed out to him how he could use some machinery to advantage, especially threshing machines—the thresher and separator were new things then, and he was a large wheat grower. He asked me if I knew where he could get any such machines, and I told him I most certainly did know because I made them.

"Don't you think I should have some?" he asked.

"Yes, I do," I answered.

"Then send me some."

He selected quite a lot of machinery from my catalogue and told me to send it on. He did not seem to be particular about the cost and left the selection largely to me. It was a large order and most welcome. It was the general habit of the wealthy Southern planters seldom to reckon the cost of anything and some of them got themselves in trouble by this financial carelessness, but not Lloyd, for he was well off and shrewd.

I rarely secured written orders for anything from our Southern customers and I did not carry any sort of a memorandum book in which to put orders. When I returned from a trip I had my orders in my head. I depended on my memory, which had been pretty well trained.

Affairs with us were going along fairly satisfactorily and we were making a reasonable amount of money when suddenly the Civil War broke and at once all of our business south of Maryland ceased. We did not have a large credit account in the seceded states as trade there was mainly for cash and it was their custom to pay promptly. But the war stopped any new business from that quarter.

The people of to-day do not know that old South or its hospitality. Here is an example:

I was driving one evening through a new country in Virginia. Night approached. There were no hotels, and I asked a man I met on the road where was the nearest good house to stop. He gave me the name of a planter, said I should know it by the high pillars and long avenue lined with trees—" Drive up there and you will be well taken care of." I reached the house before ten o'clock. It was quiet and dark, but in the negro quarters there were music and dancing. I drove down there with the buggy, which was at once taken in charge by one of the servants, who told me I should find the doors open, the dining room also open with plenty of refreshments on the sideboard, to help myself, and then go up in the hallway, peep into some room, and if there were nobody in, just make myself at home. This I did. I was warmly welcomed at the breakfast table, and spent a day or two there very pleasantly. They wanted to make me stay longer. There were plenty of good servants to do the work, a visit gave no trouble to the ladies of the house, and if the visitor was cultured and interesting he was an acceptable guest, but in any case would be hospitably entertained. I was just as much at home ten minutes after I got to the breakfast table as though I had known them a long time. I visited them again after the war broke out. The lady of the house said she wished all the Yankees had one head so she could cut it off even if she suffered eternal punishment. Shortly after she saw some Union officers riding by and, notwithstanding her recent words of hatred, said, "We must not let them pass at dinner time. Invite them in." There was no hospitality in the world like Southern hospitality.

The beginning of the Civil War did not call for any great drafts of men in our section and we had nothing like the recruiting enthusiasm that marked our entry into the war with Germany. Of course, we were all unsettled, but none of us really comprehended the sort of contest that was opening. In those days of small newspapers and of comparatively limited information from various parts of the States we, in the outlying districts—and York was only a little town—were not so alive to national events as were the people in the larger cities who had better means of communication.

Our business dropped very low and one day, coming back from a sales trip, I found that the factory had burned down the night before. The insurance rates were then very high and being insured was the exception rather than the rule. We carried practically no insurance and therefore our loss was almost total. Our creditors gathered together in a meeting, and I had two almost simultaneous surprises.

The first was that we could only muster cash

enough to pay twenty-five cents on the dollar above
the mortgages and preferred claims, and the second
was that the creditors seemed very glad to get
that much, as they had not, I learned, expected
to get anything over the mortgage. I had never
thought of settling a debt for less than its face
value, and I refused to enter into any agreement
that did not include ultimately paying everyone
in full. My partners saw no possibility of starting
up business with a great load of debt and a dis-
solution of the partnership was agreed upon. One
of the firm went to Philadelphia and the other
went West. I may say here that my active partner, W. W. Dingee, was a gentleman of great
ability and the highest character. He secured a
position with J. I. Case & Co. of Racine, Wiscon-
sin, and warmly thanked me for taking over the
debts of the firm and preserving its honour.

Our largest creditors were Messrs. P. A. & S.
Small, who were York's leading citizens. They
had the most extensive business in York and in
addition to their own claims they held proxies for
the majority of the other outside creditors. My
partners having withdrawn, Mr. Samuel Small
asked me what I proposed to do. I announced
that my plan was to have all of the creditors absolutely release the property so that I could start up
business again without any interference on account
of debts and then let me bind myself to pay within
three or four years. If they would not agree to

that plan then I should have to devise some other way, but I was afraid that any other way would delay their eventual payment.   However, I added, I was going to pay all of them in full no matter what they agreed to.

I found that Samuel Small was my staunch friend as was his partner, Philip A. Small.   As their firm was the principal creditor Samuel Small took charge of the meeting.   He said he had watched my course very closely since I had been in York and he had confidence that I should make good and therefore that he would make an exception to his general rule always in the case of a failure to take what he could get at once and charge the balance to profit and loss.   He said that instead, their firm would vote to give me a chance and do all they could to assist me.   The smaller creditors all agreed with him and thus I began business over again, this time alone and in the ruins of the old factory.   I leased a warehouse on the location of our present factory and fitted it up for a shop.

The men to whom I owed money advanced further supplies just as though they were not creditors, and I found that the very relation of creditor and debtor made them to all intents and purposes my silent partners.   Every one of them aided me in every way he could.   Within four years I paid all of their claims.   Those were four hard years.   I worked practically all of the time.   From five to seven in the morning I worked in the office.

Then I was in the shop from seven in the morning until six in the evening, and then back in the office until ten at night. But I enjoyed the work. It was a kind of play—a great game that forestalled the need for outside recreation.

The earning of our daily bread and the eating of it were then much closer together than now. If a man had a small shop, he lived over it. If he had a large shop he lived near it. There was none of that sharp distinguishing between home and office that obtains to-day. One did not close his desk and leave for the day; he was always with his business—that was his life, but, although absorbing, the business life was not so intense as is to-day's. We worked long hours but, when you consider that we had none of the modern conveniences that to-day make so many things easy to accomplish, you will realize that we spent a good part of our time in work that is to-day delegated to someone else. The steel pen was gradually taking the place of the quill, but we still blotted with sand. A man can to-day more easily do in a couple of hours all that we could do then in a day; but compressing so many of our old days into a single day makes for an intensity of work that cannot well be kept up through the long hours that we worked then. Many of the older men kill themselves by trying to work through the hours they used to work— they do not realize that the score and not the hours is what counts. It is the same with the men in the shop. Under modern conditions they should not attempt to work twelve hours a day. I am not certain that eight or any other arbitrary figure is right. It all depends upon the work. It is hard to get away from calculating work by hours instead of by results.

I did not realize until years after how really unusual it was then for creditors to permit me not merely an extension but also what amounted to a fresh start. Credits were then usually very long; it was not the length of the credit but the payment on the day due that mattered. In our town the ordinary bills were paid but once a year—April 1st. On that day the people came in from all over the county and, cash in hand, went around to clean up all their bills. The town was thronged with people—it was a kind of holiday, for the shops generally closed. If a man did not pay on that day he was as good as insolvent. We in business had to pay somewhat more often than once a year, but seldom did we pay more often than quarterly. But on the first of April we had to pay, or lose standing. We, too, paid in cash; sometimes we used bank checks for payments to distant points, but drawing a check was something of a ceremony and was reserved for the larger affairs. Even in the big cities, if a man had ten bills to pay, he would draw the cash and take it around rather than draw ten checks. In the country only a few people would accept checks. They did not regard them as payments but in the more strict legal sense of being only directions to banks to make payments. I do not recall in those early days a single case other than my own of what is now known as constructive credit. The general practice was to get what a man had the moment he failed to pay on the due date—for the old business man had a profound respect for ready money. You simply could not stay in business unless you paid your debts.

CHAPTER IV

I AM "CAPTURED" BY LINCOLN AFTER HAVING SOLD
YORK TO THE REBELS

THE beginnings of the events which developed into the Civil War did not much move us. York was distinctively Northern but not bitterly anti-Southern. The community felt that slavery was wrong in principle. At the same time, being acquainted with many slave owners, we also knew that slavery was better in practice than in theory and that the planter who was cruel to his Negroes was a rare exception. No matter what his personal disposition might be, slaves were so very expensive that it would be as ridiculous to maltreat them as to maltreat a stable of blooded horses.

The situation was not unlike that which obtains in prohibition to-day. There are fanatics on both sides. The majority of us, I think, are distinctly against the sale of intoxicating beverages and especially the saloon, but we would not wreck the country in order to enforce prohibition. That is, from a larger viewpoint, we cannot conceive the regulation of a beverage to be of such overwhelming importance as to make every other issue insignificant. There are others who would prefer a barren waste without liquor to a garden spot where the Rum Demon dwelt.

It often happens that the less you know about a subject, the more fanatical you can become. It is hard to hate a man whom you know. The fanatical abolitionists and the fanatical slave advocates did not know each other. Therefore they could hate. Some things in "Uncle Tom's Cabin," for instance, could not have been written if Harriet Beecher Stowe had resided in and been familiar with the South. John Brown's raid, which had as its object the starting of an insurrection among the slaves of Virginia, would not have taken place had he understood the slaves, for he would then have known that the Negroes did not know the meaning of revolt—that they were, in the main, more interested in three meals a day than in political theory; and that, if he had succeeded in stirring them to the point of frenzy, the only result would have been chaos.

We felt that slavery was a political question and we were more concerned with establishing the principle that all new states admitted to the Union—for then the admission of a new state was as personal a matter to every citizen as the election of a member to a small club—should be free states. We were concerned with the question that Lincoln put to Douglas at Freeport:

"Can the people of a United States territory,

in any legal way, against the will of any citizen of the United States, exclude slavery from its limits prior to the formation of a state constitution?"

The debates of Lincoln and Douglas, and Lincoln's great speech at the Cooper Institute in New York in February, 1860, fired the country. They made known the legal position of slavery and they made known to the East something of the qualities which this wonderful man had in him. His gift of clear thought and Biblical speech convinced the serious citizen, disgusted with the vacillations of Buchanan, that he was the man who might cement together the Union that seemed in a fair way to need the services of a very competent mason. For there was no doubt where Lincoln stood. We needed a strong president with plenty of common sense. And for these reasons Lincoln won the nomination and the election.

Only a very few people held him as a potentially great man—not a larger number than hail every president as great. But his speeches and declarations affected me deeply—more deeply than I can well describe. They awoke in me an admiration which, a few years later, after I had met and talked with him, developed into a reverence that has grown with the years. To-day, after having met many of the leading men in most of the countries of the world during the past half century, I believe that he was one of the few supermen. This may sound extravagant but I cannot put down my feeling toward Abraham Lincoln in less emphatic terms. When the most has been said that can be said, only a fraction of the whole man has been revealed.

When the result of Lincoln's election was made known, South Carolina, it will be remembered, in a state convention repealed the act ratifying the Constitution and seceded from the Union; and before his inauguration, Georgia, Alabama, Louisiana, Mississippi, Texas, and Florida had made like decisions. We knew that the situation was serious; but, somehow, we could not adjust our minds to civil war. Neither side really believed that there was going to be a fight. The most that any one could conceive was an insurrection—an over-sized riot. Politicians were always talking fight, anyway. President Buchanan had no effective suggestion for maintaining the Union.

Then came the inauguration, and the declaration by Lincoln—I was within a few feet of the platform, closely watching his face. I knew that he meant what he said, that his promises would be kept— that he had no purpose of interfering with the institution of slavery in the states where it existed; that he was against bloodshed and violence; but that he would protect the integrity of the Union. For the benefit of the South, he said: "You have no oath registered in Heaven to destroy the Government, while I shall have a most solemn one to preserve, protect, and defend it."

We thought that the genius and firmness of
Lincoln could find a way out. Those who live
to-day have no conception of the obstacles which
the Union had already surmounted in its organization. I was a young man with little personal experience, but all around were men who had gone
through the travail of the Union. They had seen
basic points of difference between the sections
reconciled. Politics were usually violent. In most
disputes, each side held as of course that the
other was actuated by lower motives than had
hitherto been known in the history of the human
mind and that, as far as personal character was
concerned, one would have to go back to the worst
of the Roman emperors even to get a faint idea of
the moral turpitude of the opponent. We were
accustomed to violent invective; and seldom an
election passed without a number of free-for-all
fights. What we to-day would call a shockingly
vituperative campaign would then have been
classed as mild.

We did not take the fighting gestures of the
South very seriously; and neither did they take—
excepting from the stump—our attitude as meaning much of anything. We thought it was just
another case of small boys on opposite sides of the
street and safely behind their own fences, exchang-
ing vocal notes on comparative abilities in combat.

Then came Sumter and everything changed.
That was more than a challenge to fight. It was a

struck blow. Three days later came the President's proclamation asking for 75,000 men to serve for three months and calling upon all loyal citizens "to maintain the honour, the integrity, and the existence of our national Union."

Business dropped dead. Everybody started to drill. The banks closed; they stopped specie payments. We had an unofficial moratorium. Men wanted to get everything they owned converted into money and to be ready to go out and fight. Stocks and merchandise during those first days were sold at almost any price that was offered. The proclamation called for men between eighteen and forty-five and the enlistments were largely young men under twenty-one. Thus it turned out to be a boys' war. The married men as a rule did not enlist; they were not expected to; very few even thought of doing so. And when they did try, their wives often dragged them back.

It was not that the men were unwilling to fight —far from that. But there was no idea in the beginning that the country was to fight for its life. The first call for only 75,000 men to serve three months was an indication of the official view. We were generally more concerned with the quick punishment of Americans who had dared to fire upon the Stars and Stripes than we were with getting ready for a civil war—that was still inconceivable. Indignation superseded preparation.

I was a strong Union sympathizer, but because

I had been born and educated South of the Mason and Dixon line, had many relatives there, and did most of my business in the Southern States, I came under considerable suspicion from that peculiar brand of patriotism which finds its highest expression, not in service, but in doubting the service of others. The noncombatants always hate more violently than the combatants. During the Civil War I met high officers on both sides and seldom did I detect among them the slightest personal rancor. Lincoln had not a particle of it; neither had those of his Cabinet whom I met. When Lee surrendered to Grant, an officer asked a little anxiously about what would happen to his horse, and Grant answered in a flash almost of indignation:

"Take it with you, of course. I am not a horse thief."

Having been married on September 26th, 1860, I was among those who were not expected to enlist. I provided a substitute, however, and joined with other men in a troop of volunteer cavalry—a home guard. The majority of the workmen in our shop were unmarried and most of them enlisted, but with those men remaining we could easily carry on, for there was nothing much just then to do.

One of the early acts of the Confederacy was to declare that all debts owing to Northerners by Southerners were cancelled as far as the original debtors were concerned, and payable into the Confederate Treasury. A similar statute was enacted by the Union. However, this was a gentlemen's war, and men on both sides, who liked to pay their debts, found ways to do so. A good many bills were thus paid through Canada as a sort of mutual clearing house—I received several payments in that way during the war and much of the balance owing me was paid after the war.

The cheery confidence of the opening days evaporated with the Battle of Bull Run. As the Confederate armies slowly fought their way north in their campaign, actually crossed the Pennsylvania border, and, we feared, were marching toward York, our people were very much disturbed. Valuables were sent away where practicable, and some citizens left. As the troops came nearer (General Lee's headquarters were at Fredericksburg, only forty miles away), our local volunteer or emergency cavalry company was sent out to reconnoitre. The Confederates were reported to be less than thirty miles off. It was the first time our company had ever undertaken any enterprise more specifically belligerent than a parade. Captain Nes was in charge, and, before we had gone very far, the men, unused to riding, began to grow weary.

By the time we reached Hanover, eighteen miles away, many of the nearly one hundred men who started had dropped out and were either resting or ambling homeward. As may be imagined, the discipline among this volunteer company was more than lax. The men were not enlisted, and the authority of the officers was bounded by what it pleased the privates to do. Ten or fifteen miles beyond Hanover and in the vicinity of the Confederate forces, as reported by farmers who had seen them, found only half a dozen of us left. Captain Nes suggested that we might as well all return. But that did not suit my fancy and I answered:

"I am not going back until I find what the rebels are going to do."

My horse gave out and I impressed a fresh one from a farmer, leaving my own as hostage. The rest of them returned, while I trotted onward—which may seem to those experienced in the recent Great War an uncommonly rash sort of thing to do. But I did not feel that I was in any particular danger; and I was not. I was not in uniform and, anyway, our Civil War was a fight between gentlemen. Moreover, I expected to meet old friends. The men on both sides were mainly of American stock and could not think of playing other than fair. The idea that war made it necessary to pick off a lone citizen peaceably riding along a road had no part in the American make-up. You see, none of us had been really trained to war. We were quite without those larger cultural advantages of Europe which intensify what is, I believe, there called civilization to such a degree that those qualities which we, in

our crude way, think make for decency are utterly
squeezed out. In other words, we had a strong
feeling that kicking a man in the stomach was not
uncommonly skilled boxing, but rather an evidence
of abnormality. For instance, outposts of the armies might with perfect safety camp within gun-
shot of each other; for it was not considered fair
to fire on sleeping men. In fact, I think both armies issued specific orders against this practice in
order to restrain those who were unfamiliar with
the then ethics of war.

And so I rode along, quite unafraid, and highly
interested in what I hoped to do until a picket
slouched out from the roadside to inquire casually
and with the familiar Southern drawl, as to where
I was going. He had on what would pass for a
gray uniform and I knew that I was within the
Confederate lines.

"Who is in command?" I asked.

"Fitzhugh Lee," he answered.

"Do you know if W. H. Lee is there?" I went on.
"He was a schoolmate of mine."

"I think he is," he replied. And then he gave
me very complete directions as to how to reach the
Commander's tent, and without further formality,
I rode into Headquarters, hitched my horse to a
fence, and went into the tent of General Fitzhugh
Lee. He met me cordially as a former acquaintance. I told him where I had come from and
what I had come for.

"Is it true," I asked him, "that you are going through York? I am interested because I have some property there."

"No," he answered, without the least hesitation, "we are not going through York; we may go up through the Cumberland Valley toward Harrisburg. You are in no danger."

He then asked me if I knew whether any of the family were hurt in the burning of Admiral Buchanan's house in Talbot County, Maryland, telling me that the Admiral had telegraphed him to find out if possible, and he knew I was acquainted with the Admiral. I happened to have been down in Talbot County when the fire occurred, and was able to assure him that the family were all safe and most of the contents of the house had been saved; and while I was in General Lee's tent he had this message sent over the lines to the Admiral who, I believe, was in Norfolk, Virginia.

We gossiped a few minutes more and then I started to go. General Lee gave me the password but said I would probably have no difficulty getting out of the lines, and I passed the pickets, returning without using it. After I had thanked him and started to leave, it suddenly occurred to me that perhaps I was in a confidential relation, and having no intention whatsoever to serve as a spy, I asked whether I should say anything excepting that the Confederate army would not pass through York. The General waved his hand.

"Tell them anything you choose to tell." And he added with a smile, "They will soon know anyway."

So back I rode to York picking up one or two of our soldierly company, including the Captain, exchanged my horse, much to the delight of the farmer, who said he never expected to see it again, and gave the glad tidings to the people. Then I went up to Harrisburg the same night with Captain Nes and had an audience with Governor Curtin. I told him just what I had done and received his thanks for the expedition. I told him no more, however, than I had been authorized to say by General Lee.

But this was only a breathing spell for York. General Robert E. Lee after Chancellorsville, a year later, pushed forward his army by the northern route, while from the South came Gordon and Early in the hope of striking forward into Lancaster County and forcing eastward General Meade's Army of the Potomac to defend Philadelphia.

We knew that the Confederate column was on the way toward us; for several days a steady stream of farmers and merchants with wagons loaded with merchandise had filled the Gettysburg Pike and passed on through the Borough, down the Wrightsville Pike, across the river, into Lancaster and Chester counties. To our own people were added others from Adams County and the northern part of Maryland. The railroad bridge at Wrightsville

was burned the day the Confederates reached
York.   This changed the aspect of the Confederate
invasion of Pennsylvania and made Gettysburg the
mark of the flood tide of the Confederacy.

On the morning of Saturday, the 27th of June,
1863, we were informed that the Confederate army
would probably be in York that night, or at the
latest, the next morning. The leading citizens went
into session in the counting room at P. A. & S.
Small's hardware store. The Smalls, as I have
said before, were the big people of the town and
David Small, one of the proprietors of the York
Gazette, was Chief Burgess.   Among others in the
meeting were W. Latimer Small, General George
Hay, Samuel and Philip Small, Thomas E. Cochran,
(an attorney), Thomas White, and other leading
citizens who had formed a Committee of Public
Safety.

The Committee was discussing plans for the
safety of the citizens and property of the town
when I entered the meeting and proposed that it
would be well to meet the Confederates before they
entered the town—that we could make a good deal
better bargain with them then than we could after
they saw how little of our property we had been
able to remove to a place of safety. The attorney,
Mr. Cochran, said my plan would be good enough
if we could find anyone to go, if we could make
any bargain, and if the Confederates would keep
the bargain when it had been made. I told him

I would go, that I believed I could make an arrangement, and that I was certain they would keep faith as I knew the character of the men in charge. My plan, however, was not seriously entertained. Then I told them I would take the responsibility of going anyhow—which I did.

I therefore hitched up my buggy and started off. I struck the Confederate lines beyond Abbotstown, eighteen miles out, and was fortunate in meeting and old classmate, Lieutenant Redik, from Georgia, whom I had not seen since school days.

He greeted me with the words, "Hello, Farquhar. What are you doing up here among the Yankees?"

I replied, "I came just to find out what you are doing up here among the Yankees. I have some property in York and I don't want it burned. Who is in command?"

"General Gordon," he answered, "whom you may know, and General Early."

I asked him to put somebody else in charge of his company, jump into the buggy with me, and we would go to see Gordon—which he did. The General was exceedingly courteous. I did not know General Gordon personally but I knew him well through mutual friends. And, having stated exactly the object of my mission, I said:

"General Gordon, unless you have entirely changed from the character you used to have, you are neither a horse thief nor a bank robber, and fighting is more in your line than sacking a city."

He evidently knew what I had in mind and smilingly admitted that perhaps I was right. He asked me what I would have him do. I said:

"You and your men enter York quietly and then you sit down and make requisitions for whatever you reasonably want and our committee will see that they are honoured."

He thought for a second and then answered that he would be more than glad to make any arrangement that would spare the non-combatants of the town from the horrors of war, adding, "We have been treated badly down the Valley, but General Lee is not inclined to retaliate." I wrote down in my memorandum book what he said and asked him to sign it so that I could relieve the minds of the people of York. At that he was inclined to balk, but when I explained that it was not because I doubted his word but only to satisfy the Committee, especially the women of the town, who were very uneasy, he at once signed what I had written, which was to the effect that when his troops entered York and its vicinity they would not take private property or molest any one, but that they would expect some necessary supplies which we agreed to furnish.

Getting back was not quite so easy, for I did not ask for passwords as I had done the year before, remembering that I had not made use of them then, and the only thing that my friend Redik could advise was that, if any one tried to stop me, to give my horse rein and take my chances. I had no trouble until I reached the outpost. My horse was fast, and like a streak we went by the outpost and were a hundred yards away before the sentries waked up to the fact that I ought to have been stopped, and started to shoot. But I imagine that they could not have been over-anxious to get me, for among the Confederate soldiers were always enough mountain marksmen to make sure of their quarry as far as a rifle bullet would carry.

Anyway, I came through and so did the horse, without a scratch. I presented my agreement to the Committee of Safety who were still in session. They seemed to think the agreement was too good to be true and the attorney, lawyer-like, argued that if they discovered that I was not authorized by the Committee to make the agreement, the Confederates would not feel bound to carry out their promises. In reply to this I suggested that the Chief Burgess and several of the prominent citizens should ride back with me and go over the particulars with General Gordon and have it confirmed.

The Smalls joined me in insisting that a committee be appointed with full authority to arrange the terms, and that same evening, David Small (Chief Burgess), General George Hay, Latimer Small, Thomas White, and myself, as this committee, went out to the Gettysburg Pike bearing a flag of truce and entered the Confederate lines at

Farmer's Post Office which is about eight miles west of York, where they had encamped for the night. We were taken to General Gordon and again I met Lieutenant Redik who whispered to me that he had been under arrest for having let me pass out of the lines without giving the password. General Gordon was a little more formal than in the morning, but said the terms as agreed with me would be carried out, and the particulars would be arranged by General Early the next morning when he entered the town.

It was late when we got back to York and we adjourned to meet the full committee in the morning. That was Sunday. By the time the church bells were ringing, bugle calls also were coming out of the distance, and by ten o'clock General Gordon and his cavalry had arrived in Center Square, taken down the Stars and Stripes, raised the Stars and Bars, and gone on through to· Wrightsville. In a little while the infantry came up, commanded by General Early and staff. The General wore a new gray uniform and black slouch hat with a black ostrich feather. He went immediately to the Courthouse where the Committee was already in session and formally presented these two requests:

165 barrels of flour or 28,000 pounds of baked bread, 3,500 pounds of sugar, 1,650 pounds of coffee, 300 gallons of molasses, 1,200 pounds of salt, 32,000 pounds of fresh beef or 21,000 pounds of bacon or pork, the above to be delivered

at the market place on Main Street at 4 P. M. Signed by
William W. Thornton, Captain, A. C. S.

2,000 pairs of shoes or boots, 1,000 pairs of socks, 1,000
felt hats and $100,000 in United States money. Signed
by C. E. Snodgrass, Major and Chief-Quartermaster, Early's
division, approved by J. A. Early, Major-General in command. Signed June 28, 1863.

Our committee could not furnish all the money
and supplies out of hand and General Early said
that he was willing to wait a reasonable time. He
set up his headquarters in the Sheriff's office. Our
sub-committee set out to canvass the town for
money and goods to fill the order. The General
had specified United States money but we argued
that he should take Confederate money, a dollar
of which was worth about 10 cents in Federal
money—for we soon found that we could not raise
as much as $100,000 in cash. We compromised
on $28,610, as finally collected, in Federal legal
tender, and about its equivalent in merchandise.
We gave him a due bill for the balance which of
course was never collected. The Committee gave
receipts for the contributions and these later were
assumed by the Borough and paid off out of the
proceeds of a special tax.

The money was not so easily gathered, although
by Monday we had made very fair progress. General Early was not satisfied and threatened to
burn the Northern Central Railway property and
the shops adjoining in which cars were being built

for the Government.   I was, however, told personally there was no danger of the threat being carried
out.   Samuel Small, David Small, and myself
tried to convince him that this act would be a
violation of the agreement.   In the midst of this
discussion came a dispatch from General Ewell to
General Early stating that troops were concentrat-
ing near Gettysburg where they expected to make
a stand, and he was ordered to join them, General
Gordon's advance having been recalled from
Wrightsville.   He issued orders at once, and by
five o'clock the next morning the last of the Confederates were out of York and on their way to
join Lee at Gettysburg.

They had scrupulously kept to their agreement
and York was unharmed.   I followed on to the
Battle of Gettysburg as a member of the Hospital
Service—and of which more later.

When I returned from that great battle, thankful,
as we all were, that the Confederates had been
turned back, and expecting to share that joy, I had
no sooner passed into the town than I noticed
people pointing at me and jeering, calling me rebel.
At first I could not make out what it was all about.
Then I learned that after the news of Lee's 'defeat
had reached town the pinchbeck patriots had
crawled out of their holes and decided that our
Committee, instead of saving the town, had sold it
to the Confederates and that I, as the man who
had opened the negotiations, was something near

to being a traitor! I shall never forget those days, being pointed out as "the man who had sold York" to the Rebels, instead of one of those who had saved it. The accusation was ridiculous and unjust, but my indignation knew no bounds. I knew that I had helped save the city from possible ruin, not sold it. I determined to put the case before one who I knew would be just—the President.

I went to Washington, talked over the whole matter with the President's secretary, young John Hay—later our able Secretary of State, whom I knew personally. He declared that I had done exactly right and deserved public commendation.

He tried to persuade me not to insist on seeing the President, who he said was overworked and very much worried, but on second thoughts told me that the President would leave the front door of the White House at half past four to go to the War Department to meet some officers; that I could walk with him without taking up any of his time.

I took up my position on the front portico of the White House which, I noticed, particularly needed paint. There were no guards or soldiers about and no flunkeys or attendants. Several generals passed to and fro while I was there but there was nothing to prevent any one from going by the East Room to the President's office. Exactly at half past four the President came out.

Since I had seen him at his first inauguration his

face had grown sadder but his eye even more kindly. And he had taken on a kind of simple, majestic dignity that seemed more of the soul than of the person—a dignity and a majesty that one felt rather than saw. No painting, no statue, no attempt at re-creation of him on the stage, has ever given even a suggestion of this surrounding quality, of this atmosphere that came from him and lifted him away from the rut of ordinary mortals. I was almost overcome with a feeling of reverence at the sight of him. He asked as we shook hands:

"Well, sonny, what are you after?"

He did not smile, but he took my hand in his great, strong palm, placed the other on my shoulder and looked down into my face. And then I told, or maybe I blurted out, my whole story. He said nothing at all, and, when I had finished, he started on his way. I fell in beside him answering his inquiring look with:

"I am going with you; I want your advice, and to know what you think of our action."

Thus we walked together, although it took two of my steps to match his stride. He shambled just a little, as might a man who is not wholly conscious that he has a body, but I remember that he was very clean and so was his clothing, although it hung loose and ill-fitting about him. He wore a soft, black, slouch hat. Some pictures give the idea that Lincoln was ungainly. His hands and his feet were large but not ungainly; not a motion was ungraceful. Great and strong and rugged, he was—with the greatness and strength and ruggedness of the glorious live oak.

As we walked he asked me questions: Was I married? Did I have any children? Had I a business in York? What kind was it? Was it prosperous?

And thus we walked up the steps to the War Department Building and through to a room where were already together the Secretary of War Stanton and perhaps half a dozen generals. Stanton was personally known to me, my cousin, James Hallowell, being his private secretary. I had met him several times. The President, giving my hand a squeeze, brought me before the Secretary as he said:

"Stanton, I have captured that young chap who sold York, Pennsylvania, to the Rebels. What are we going to do with him?"

CHAPTER V

THE BUSINESS SIDE OF WAR

ALTHOUGH President Lincoln's voice, as he asked Secretary Stanton what he should do with me, gave no evidence that he was not asking a serious question and expecting a serious answer, I felt, nervous as I was, that he had already given his decision and I was not surprised when the Secretary answered just as gravely:

"We ought to promote him."

And then he went on to say that by my action some millions of dollars' worth of property had probably been saved at a trifling cost and that I deserved very high commendation. The President nodded at this, and, turning to me, said:

"You were wise not to neglect an opportunity to be of service. Opportunity does not knock at a man's door every day. The mistake you made was in worrying yourself over what people say about you. You should go through life doing what you believe to be right and not bother yourself over what people may say. They will soon forget their criticisms."

"The place for you," he continued, "is in the army. It is a place I should love to take myself.

I will follow you up and see that you get a chance for promotion. The mustering officer is right here."

I told him that the situation at home with my family and my business would make it all but impossible for me to enter the army unless we were in an actual emergency. As things were, I felt that I could be of more service at home. I told him that I had served with the emergency men at Gettysburg, and had furnished a substitute.

He smiled gently as he answered:

"Being married is no excuse. But you, may be, are contributing your mite and that is all any of us can do."

"I wish my mite could be spelled 'm-i-g-h-t,'" I answered.

"Might is made up of mites—so what is the difference?" he replied. "Our aim in life should be to leave the world a mite better than we found it, and the only way we can do that is to contribute a little every day. You can go home and tell them what I have said to you; tell them that you have my thanks and the thanks of the Government."

The news of my interview had preceded me and I was received cordially when I went back home, and never again heard about having "sold York."

It would seem that the President talked in platitudes. As far as words were concerned, he did. But a platitude is something that one utters as by rote and that Lincoln did not do. His nature was a simple, fundamental one and he really thought in the powerful, elemental way that is expressed in what are almost copy-book maxims. Others might say such things off-hand. Lincoln lived them. The next time I saw him was just before the marvellous Gettysburg speech. A small party of us drove up to Gettysburg early in the morning and just as Lincoln was mounting his horse from Lawyer Wills' home, where he stopped, to ride up to Cemetery Hill, I had a chance to shake hands with him. He remembered me and spoke a half-joking word or two.

He had become graver than when I had seen him in Washington. The terrific strain that he had been under showed in the deepening lines in his face and the abyss of sadness in his eyes. Time has idealized the President. For me he never needed idealization. But those who know the days of the Civil War only from books can have but little realization of the tense political struggles that were taking place in the North—of the personal opposition to the President on the part of the extreme Abolitionists on the one hand and the Copperheads on the other, and of the movement led by the *Tribune* among them to force him out. They wanted to displace Lincoln with someone else whose sole thought would be the abolishing of slavery rather than the saving of the Union.

The Gettysburg and Vicksburg victories immensely helped the President but they by no means silenced all the virulent attacks against him. There was not a general slogan of "Stand behind the President" in those days.

I stood very near to the speaker's stand. Edward Everett made an oration. It was eloquent but it was long, and the President, as he sat there, looked very, very weary. Then the time came for him to move to the rustic platform where he was to speak. The place is marked now by a monument on which is inscribed his great address. He rose slowly, and as he took his place in the centre of the platform, he drew from his waistcoat pocket what appeared to me to be a small, discoloured leaf torn from a memorandum book, and, glancing at it now and then, delivered slowly, clearly, dwelling on each phrase as though he were pronouncing a benediction, these words:

Fourscore and seven years ago our fathers brought forth upon this continent a new nation, conceived in liberty, and dedicated to the proposition that all men are created equal.

Now we are engaged in a great civil war, testing whether that nation, or any nation so conceived and so dedicated, can long endure. We are met on a great battlefield of that war. We have come to dedicate a portion of that field, as a final resting-place for those who here gave their lives that that nation might live. It is altogether fitting and proper that we should do this.

But, in a larger sense, we cannot dedicate, we cannot consecrate, we cannot hallow, this ground. The brave men, living and dead, who struggled here, have consecrated it far above our poor power to add or detract. The world will little note, nor long remember what we say here, but it can never forget what they did here. It is for us the living, rather to be dedicated here to the unfinished work which they who fought here have thus far so nobly advanced. It is rather for us to be here dedicated to the great task remaining before us, that from these honoured dead we take increased devotion to that cause for which they gave the last full measure of devotion; that we here highly resolve that these dead shall not have died in vain; that this nation, under God, shall have a new birth of freedom; and that government of the people, by the people, for the people, shall not perish from the earth.

It was over so quickly; it was so direct, so simple, so forceful, that practically none of those in the audience seemed to realize that they had just heard the most glorious joining of word and thought that has ever come from mortal man—that we had been given the opportunity to hear the whole philosophy and spirit and courage and reason for the United States being put into the compass of the Lord's Prayer—that the words we had heard would be to-day in every true American home and office in the land; and that no one hunting for a definition for that new word "Americanism" need go beyond those sentences.

Perhaps it was because I knew and venerated Lincoln that I was more deeply impressed than by any words that I had ever heard uttered during my lifetime. Turning to those with me I said: "When this battle becomes a misty memory those words will be remembered"—which was received with a doubtful smile.

Edward Everett, turning to the President and either because he was courteous or because the address had moved him, or because of both, said in my hearing:

"Mr. President, you have made a great speech. My address will be remembered only because it was made on the same day."

The President answered: "The audience does not seem to agree with you."

The audience certainly did not. They did not really know what they had heard. When a great thing happens, those who are there rarely have any notion of the greatness. The *Tribune* said that the President had "made a few remarks" and a Harrisburg paper, published the next morning, spoke sneeringly of it as being unworthy of a president. About a year later at an agricultural meeting at Elkton, Maryland, I spoke to Horace Greeley about this and he gruffly answered:

"One of the many times we were damn fools" —and I told him I forgave him.

I heard the President's inaugural in the following year and that was the last time I saw him alive. By the time of Lincoln's second inauguration his position had become more permanent. The personal opposition to him was negligible. But it was not until April 15, 1865, with the war ended, and Abraham Lincoln suddenly dead, that the country began to know what it had had and what it had lost in the way of a man. We feel a good deal the same way about Theodore Roosevelt, another great, clean, courageous American. The world seems a lonesome place since he has gone. It is a great country that can produce such men.

Now let us go back a little—back to the day when the Confederates left York on the summons of Lee to help him check Meade. We knew that a great battle was impending. In a little while we learned that it had begun on the hills about Gettysburg. I was always interested in hospital practice and the best way that I knew of to be of help was in the Hospital Corps. I drove up to Gettysburg in my buggy, being enabled to pass through the Confederate lines by using the passes given me by Generals Gordon and Early some days before. On the second day of the battle, I entered that part of the Union lines which was in command of General Kilpatrick. Having been seen coming out of the Confederate lines, I was arrested, but fortunately, as I seldom go anywhere without meeting someone I know, a soldier who knew me told the officer by whom I had been arrested that I was all right. The officer said:

"Then you had better see General Kilpatrick mighty quick. He is just about fifty yards away. You run for him and I will follow."

I jumped out of my buggy and started for the General, the officer closely following. After saluting, my officer friend told the General my mission, and upon hearing my reason for being

there and how I got there, and remarking gruffly:
"If you are an imposter, you are more dangerous
than Jeff Davis," he not only released me, but
permitted me to join his division in the Medical
Corps.

It was evening. During the night General
Kilpatrick threw himself on the ground, saying,
"I am going to get an hour or two's sleep; wake
me up when I am wanted." I needed sleep badly
too, and I lay down by him with my head across
his knees. He asked, "What in the —— are you
doing?" I told him nobody was going to take
the trouble to wake me up, but when they woke
him I would be on hand for any emergency. We
were at once fast asleep. It seemed but a few
moments afterward, although it might have
been several hours, when the Louisiana Tigers
made their attack. My horse and buggy were
taken to care for the wounded, and although
Major Van Voorhees gave me a receipt for them,
I have never seen them since. Capt. H. B. Blood,
Assistant Quartermaster, wrote me after the battle
that he had found the wreck of a buggy with some
papers under the seat showing that it had belonged
to me.

The best makeshift for a hospital I could find
was a big shed with a hayloft above, and there the
wounded and dying soldiers were stretched out on
the ground side by side. As the surgeons were
engaged elsewhere and there seemed to be no one

in command, I took charge myself. We could do but little for the poor fellows except give them water and make their lot perhaps a little easier until they died or came under a doctor's care.

While we were caring for the wounded soldiers, a number of cavalrymen rode up and began to throw some hay down from the loft above, scattering dust upon the wounded, and I ordered them to stop. They did not question my authority.

About two o'clock in the afternoon of the next day—the third day of the battle—there commenced a tremendous cannonade of some three hundred guns in one great battery, to clear the way for a charge on which the Confederates were to stake their all. They did not have enough ammunition to keep the artillery going as long as they had hoped, I learned afterward. Anyway, the cannonade ceased and then began a terrific din—the rattle of small arms, shouts, yells, orders—for Pickett and his men were making their famous charge up Cemetery Hill. I saw the men rushing forward and dropping, wave after wave, each wave gaining a few rods over the last. And then they stopped and seemed almost to clutch, as does a drowning man at a stick, and went down. They were near enough for me to see their faces, and I shall never forget that sight. This time they did not come up again. The waves ebbed; our men ceased to fire; the charge was over—and a failure. The Battle of Gettysburg was won. The Confederate soldiers who reached our lines and were made prisoners, were treated with great kindness by our men, given water out of Federal canteens, and loudly cheered, several of our boys crying, "Welcome back into the Union." After the strain of battle won there was a great lifting of spirits, and a disposition to forgive and forget. In war, it is said, only those who are not in the fighting lines are good haters. When attending the 50th anniversary of the Battle of Gettysburg, I met a Confederate and a Union soldier standing together on Cemetery Hill discussing the charge. One remarked, "Fifty years ago we would not have been talking together as two friends at this spot," and I interjected: "Oh, yes, you would," and told them of the Union soldiers handing the Confederates water to drink out of their canteens.

The Potomac was in flood, and Lee, retreating toward it, short of ammunition, could have been captured had the victory been followed up. At least, so some of Meade's generals thought, and I well remember the disgust of General Wadsworth of New York (the father of Senator Wadsworth). He declared bitterly:

"I left a wife and children at home—everything. Now here is a chance of ending this war and they are throwing it away."

Some time later, when General Grant had been ordered east to take command of the Army of the

Potomac, I had the chance of meeting him. I was stopping at the Jones House in Harrisburg and was informed that the General would probably arrive at one o'clock at night and would stop over to rest until morning. Feeling very sure from my knowledge of him that he would do no such thing, I went down to the station to wait for him, and met him as he came in. He ordered a train to go on to Washington, but while arrangements were being made I had. at least an hour with him. I found him very tired, covered with soot from his long journey, but wholly calm and very approachable. He wanted to talk about Gettysburg and was very much interested in my account of that battle. He agreed that it was a great mistake not to have followed up Lee and said that, if the battle had been pressed and he had been allowed to finish his cleaning up in the West, the war would have been very materially shortened.

For even after Gettysburg, we were not certain of victory and the generals of the Army of the Potomac did not, in the beginning, understand Grant. After the war one of his generals related to me the following instance of Grant's magnanimity. He said that when a number of them heard of his plans for the capture of Vicksburg, they were so certain of failure that they drew up a round-robin of protest and telegraphed to President Lincoln. Within twenty-four hours

Grant had ordered the charge and by night probably the most important victory of the war had been won. That evening the "round-robin" generals gathered in a tent, giving orders to the sentry that no one was to be admitted. They did not know what was going to become of them. They had sent their message to the President but events had proved that Grant had been absolutely right and they had been absolutely wrong. There seemed no reason in the world why all of them should not be court-martialled for insubordination. It was a glum party. There apparently was no hope; they were sitting down silently and dejectedly gazing blankly at each other, when a man smoking a cigar walked past the sentry into the tent. Looking around, he remarked:

"You look as though you were having a funeral."

It was General Grant. The tension broke and the whole group almost collapsed. Then one of them confessed to General Grant what they had done. He listened with an amused smile, and taking the telegram from his pocket remarked:

"If that dispatch could have left our field office without my knowledge I would be as great a failure as you seemed to think me. That is the reason I ordered the charge a little earlier than I had intended. You have made a grave mistake, but I forgive you. Just forget it, as I shall."

The general who related this to me in strict confidence as to his name, said:

"Is it any wonder we worshipped General Grant?"

Afterward I came to know General Grant well and became very fond of him. It has been my fortune to know all of the presidents since Lincoln. But of that later.

The business conduct of the Civil War was not without its dark side. While, of course, there are many who would scorn to enrich themselves by taking advantage of the Government's necessities during the cruel strain of war, it is nevertheless notoriously true that the vultures gather where there is a chance for good pickings, and it was true of the Civil War, just as it has been more or less true of nearly all wars. In a number of cases an account of the people who sold supplies to the Government during the Civil War would be little better than a record of crime. When I compare the record then with the record of the present it is to draw from that comparison a picture of the increase in business honesty that has come about with the years.

In the World War we made many mistakes. Many things cost the Government much more than they should have cost, but a small minority of those who sold to the Government were shameless profiteers and still fewer tried to impose bad goods. Nearly everyone who made anything for the Government during the World War had a feeling of personal responsibility and, where what they made was not up to standard, it was my experience that, as a rule, it was due only to a lack of knowledge of the proper process. And there never was a valid criticism upon the splendid body of dollar-a-year men who supplied the purchases.

In the Civil War the Government did not require, as compared with to-day, vast quantities of supplies. And as war then was not the very intricate affair that it has since become, these supplies called for comparatively few new processes and did not make any great strain upon the nation. Even the limited manufacturing resources of that time had by no means to turn wholly to war. So supplying the Government was more or less an affair of those who chose to undertake that sort of work. Army contracting became a business of itself. Many unprincipled men were attracted to it in the hope of cheating the Government, and some succeeded. It is particularly reprehensible for men deliberately and shamelessly to profiteer at the expense of suffering humanity during the throes of war; but there were such, for whom the hangman's noose would be a fitting punishment.

In some cases the contractors formed rings which included government inspectors so that not only was it practically impossible for an outsider to sell at all to the Government, but it was possible for an insider to sell trash. It is safe to say that a number of Union soldiers went to their deaths because a few men thought more of money than they did of life, or honour, or any of those qualities that decent men esteem. I ran into this ring and I beat it.

My business being very slack, I went to Washington to see what I could do on government contracts. Walking through one of the warehouses filled with goods for the hospitals, I was shocked by their poor quality. Many of the chairs had been simply slung together. I saw stretchers that would not bear the weight of a man. It filled me with indignation to think that in our country were men with so little conscience that they could make such rubbish, let alone impose it upon the Government with an utter disregard of the fact that they might thereby be destroying human life.

Having always been inclined to go to headquarters I went to the office of the Medical Purveyor, General Sutherland, told him what I had seen, and said I would like to send down a sample of my own work. He gave me a small order which I filled with the very best material and shipped to Washington. One of my friends told me that I should find my goods condemned; that it was impossible to get an order through excepting with the consent of the ring. And, sure enough, the formal notification came back that my whole shipment had been condemned. I took the next train to Washington, went to the warehouse, found my wares shoved back into a corner and then, looking around among the goods that had been passed, picked out a lot of samples. I will admit that I used no uncommon care to pick out the best of the other goods, but what I did pick out had been passed by the government inspectors and therefore were officially better than mine.

Having arranged my little exhibit, I went up to see General Sutherland. A clerk tried to keep me out. The ring went so far as to prevent to the best of its ability any outsider reaching the head of the department. But I knocked his hand away and forced my way in to the General. He was in a bad humour, had just received news that a soldier friend of his, wounded in the back, had been killed by the breaking of a litter, and he bitterly turned to me:

"It seems that your goods are no better than the others."

"Perhaps not," I answered, "but I expected them to be condemned. I would like you to come down with me to the warehouse and see for yourself."

This, of course, was a very unusual request to a busy department head. But I think that he had taken a fancy to me, and also that he felt that something might be wrong; so he went down with me to my exhibit. I laid one of the litters out of the approved stock across two chairs and asked him to sit on it. That litter, I knew, had a big knot in its rail. As I expected, it broke under his weight. I got one of my litters and asked him to try it. He did so gingerly; then I jumped on it and called one of the attendants to come and jump on it with me. I knew that my rails had been made of clear white hickory and that they would stand anything. I took a couple of chairs out of the passed stock. The General broke them in his hands. I gave him one of my own chairs and asked him to try to find some way to break it. He sat on it, he jumped on it, and finally threw it high up in the air and let it fall. He could not hurt it and I knew that he could not.

Then he called the inspector who had condemned my goods and gave him the most terrific lecture I have ever heard; said that he ought to be court-martialled and thrown out of the place. He gave me a large order and, because he knew that the ring would make it just as inconvenient as possible for me and among other annoyances hold up my payments to force me out of business, he insisted that each bill be sent to him personally, and he sent me his own personal checks drawn on the Treasury of the United States, till the close of the war.

After the war was over, I wanted to make General Sutherland a present of some kind as an evidence of my regard. I had a bureau made in the factory and shipped it to him as a wedding present—for he married when the war ended. In a little while I received a very courteous note thanking me for the bureau, complimenting me on its workmanship—and enclosing a check. He said that he had had a cabinet-maker appraise the article and, although he was very glad indeed to be remembered, he would prefer to pay for it. For, he went on, although he knew my work with the Department was entirely finished and that I expected no favours of any kind, he wanted to keep his hands spotlessly clean.

I ran into many examples of ring contracting. I took up with Secretary Stanton a number of specific instances which I thought he ought to know about. To my surprise, he said that he was entirely familiar with what was going on.

"The whole thing," he said, "is rotten clear through. Why, you may not know it, but we even have officers down in the South who are speculating in cotton. I am collecting evidence everywhere; but as things now are, I think the Government would lose more than it would gain if I went into these frauds."

After the war there were some prosecutions of the more flagrant offenders and it is most unfortunate that more of them could not have been gaoled, but I think, on the whole, Secretary Stanton was right in deciding that he would do better to give his first attention to prosecuting the war rather than to the criminals incident thereto.

The organization for war was so imperfect and there were so few trained men to assist, that the burden of conducting from behind the lines fell very heavily on the heads of departments. That was before the day when people understood the delegation of responsible authority. There was much suffering for necessaries, even food and clothing—a striking contrast to the abundant supplies furnished our soldiers in the recent World War.

As far as the North was concerned, the drain upon the man power was not serious. When conscription went into effect and men might be called between the ages of eighteen and forty-five, at first any man called was permitted, instead of serving, to pay to the Government a sum of money. Most men with families did this. But then the Government got so much depreciated money and so few soldiers that they had to change the plan and if one did not desire to serve he had to provide a substitute. Little difficulty was discovered in getting substitutes at anywhere from $300 to $700 or $800 in cash. Where a large proportion of the men in an election district were drafted, the fee for substitutes was high; where there were plenty of men over, the fee was low. It was a common thing for communities to collect a fund to pay substitutes to relieve their district from the draft. Many of those were expecting to volunteer anyway and simply took the substitute money as an additional bounty. In the South the conscription age extended to fifty, and, since they were compelled to call on practically their entire man power, they felt the war, other things being equal, much more severely than did the North.

We did not particularly feel the expense of the war. We had a small tax on incomes over $1,000, a sales tax which did not last long, and bonds, of which the Government issued, for then, very large quantities, which were absorbed almost entirely by financial interests under the lead of Jay Cooke. It is true there were advertisements of these bonds and those who had money could buy them, but the average man did not buy. Buying was not presented to him as a duty. I think it may safely be said that those who bought did so, not so much from a sense of duty as for investment purposes. This does not apply, of course, to the larger financiers who understood the desperate straits in which the Government was for money. Many of the great banks bought bonds that they did not want. But between the bankers generally and the Treasury Department there was not at all a close coöperation. Otherwise the greenbacks need not have been issued.

Prices advanced, although to nothing like such

an extent as in the recent war: and we had that disparity between gold and paper which other countries now have but which we, to-day, know nothing of. For instance, at times it took $2.50 in greenbacks to buy one gold dollar. Gold remained the standard and thus we had a double method of reckoning. Gold was used to pay our import duties and the Government paid the coupons of its bonds in gold, but otherwise the greenback was the legal tender.

The workman who before the war had been receiving $1.25 a day in gold, after the war received double that in greenbacks, but in gold little more than he formerly received. But we did not then have that curious world-wide phenomenon of the present, in which men generally, working for high wages, are insisting upon doing less work. The men returning from the Civil War, as far as my experience went, were anxious to go to work. They turned to in my shop with a will—glad to get back and glad to have something useful to do. There was work for everyone because, with the close of the war, and the return of the soldiers after the last great review in Washington, the country began to hum with business. A large number of returning soldiers took up land in the West, and all went merrily till the great panic of 1873.

CHAPTER VI

BUILDING UP AFTER THE CIVIL WAR

BETWEEN the conditions at the close of the Civil War and the conditions at the close of the World War are indeed some points of similarity. We had fairly high prices and about the same number of soothsayers predicting that prices immediately would drop and that there would be a return to pre-war conditions. As I look back over all these years in business, it seems to me that the general sentiment has always been that we were going to return sometime or other to something or other, but that under no circumstances do we ever return to exactly the same condition!

We had extravagances then, but not on the scale of the present day. I do not know whether that was because there were then not so many things to buy or because people were not so gifted in extravagance. Simple habits still held them. Within a little while came the enormous stimulation of the opening of the West. The resources of the country had never really been developed. The war had not grazed them. Men were needed for the building of railways; they were needed everywhere in constantly increasing numbers, for we were beginning that tremendous expansion on inflated money which culminated in the panic of 1873.

But there was practically nothing of that which we know to-day as "labour unrest." The restlessness took itself out in doing work—not in avoiding it. And, judging from the men in my own factory, I should say that their per-man production increased after the war. This, I believe, was the condition all over the country. In fact we produced so much goods that in many lines we were ahead of the facilities for distribution and hence ahead of the consumption of the country, and had distinct "over-production." I hold that "over-production" is only bad distribution. Many people speculated in government securities and in greenbacks. I had a friend in Holland who bought bonds at 45 cents on the dollar in gold and later sold them at 105 in gold.

This revival of business did not begin the day after peace. It took some little while to get going, but it was a question of months not of years, for, fortunately, we were not burdened with "reconstructors" of the universe as after the late war. The only section that had the misfortune to be "reconstructed" was the South. Had it not been for the assassination of Lincoln, I think that the prosperity of the country would, in spite of the decline in man power in the South, have been

general.   For that great man, as the war was near-
ing its close, had already evolved plans, not for the
punishment of the South, but for getting it back
into the fold again.   Lincoln was not a man who
could hold a personal grudge.   But it was different
with President Johnson.   I knew him slightly and,
although I try to think well of everyone, I never,
then or since, have been able to think well of him.
He, too, had risen from a humble origin but, unlike
Lincoln, had been narrowed instead of broadened
by his experiences.   Almost his first words as
President were these:

"The American people must be taught to know
and understand that treason is a crime . . .
it must not be regarded as a mere difference of
political opinion.   It must not be excused as an
unsuccessful rebellion to be overlooked and forgotten."

He sobered greatly with responsibility, but in
the beginning he was very radical and was intent
on the punishment of the South rather than on the
betterment of the whole country.

In this he was supported by many members of
Congress who could not appreciate the larger view
of Lincoln or of General Grant.   For Grant, too,
was a man who believed that a fight is a fight and
that when it is over, it is over.   Johnson's attitude
created many clashes.   One day I happened to be
in Washington stopping at the Willard Hotel (on
the same site as the present New Willard).   Gen-

eral Grant was sitting in the lobby. An aide
rushed in and whispered something to him. Hur-
riedly the General ran out, jumped on his horse,
and galloped away. I knew that something unusual must be in the air and went over to the
War Department to get the news from Stanton's
Secretaries, Colonel Pelloze, and my cousin James
Hallowell. They told me that a plan had been
afoot to arrest General Lee and that General
Grant, hearing of it, had gone at once to President
Johnson and informed him that Lee had surrendered to him at Appomattox Court House and that
he had there told him that he would not be disturbed at all, but was free to go ahead and help
reconstruct his country. And therefore, so Grant
informed the President, the army was going to
see that these terms were carried out, and intimated
that if any one attempted to disturb Lee he would
find himself under arrest. That, I believe, was
the last of Johnson's idea of arresting Lee.

Most of my business having been with the
South, I began to receive inquiries from some of
my old customers who were trying to get back into
business. For instance, Captain Borum, of the
firm of Borum and McLean, who was the
largest merchant in my line in Norfolk, but who
had closed up his business during the war and
acted as Provost Marshal for Virginia, told me that
he wanted to start up again. He owed me a considerable sum. He had no money—none of them

had any money. I told him that I would give him no trouble on that score and I went down to Norfolk and he invited me to dinner at his home. His sister was at the table with us and in the conversation it developed that I came from Pennsylvania. She asked abruptly:

"Are you from Pennsylvania?"

I admitted that I was. Without a word, she got up and walked away. But a child of four or five years old in the room was not so easily convinced.

"You ain't a Yankee, are you?" she demanded, "'cause they got horns."

None of the small children in the South had ever seen what their parents called a "Yankee," and I think that they very generally imagined that Yankees were animals quite different from the ordinary human animal. Probably the children in Germany and Austria and France all gained similar ideas of their particular enemies.

My host was considerably embarrassed by the incident but it only amused me. I chuckled some months later when I heard that this same lady had married a Yankee colonel!

In all of my journeyings through the South immediately after the war I did not find any great bitterness excepting among some of the women. The men were inclined to acknowledge that they were whipped and to accept conditions. This is not to say that they were at all happy about the result—far from it—but the intense feeling against

the North developed out of the reconstruction—
so-called—and not out of the war.

There were comparatively few able-bodied men
about on my first journey to the South. Those
who had formerly been rich had shoes, but most
of the population, black and white, were barefooted.
They had plenty of corn bread and some bacon,
but that is all they did have. Their only money
was in the worthless Confederate issues. The
houses and plantations were run down. During
the war there had been nobody to repair them.
Now there was no money to pay any one to repair.
They were clean; they had the same air as before.
But no silver was to be seen—no luxuries—none of
the dinners that we would call banquets, which formerly were the usual affair of the Southern planter.

At many of the places I visited the Negroes did
not understand their freedom; they were in their
old places on the farms, many of them being
given work on shares, as there was no money to
pay them wages. A large export tax on cotton
(afterward abrogated as unconstitutional) made
the prospects of a crop return very slight, but even
had it been otherwise, they were not equipped to
raise crops. They had neither fertilizers nor tools.
Nearly every bit of iron had been absorbed for
military use and it was a common sight to see a
Negro ploughing with a piece of iron fastened to a
forked stick. The Negroes generally called their
employers "master." There was no race hatred

and I did not notice any in the South until it became apparent that the law that no one might vote without first taking the oath of allegiance had handed the Government over to the Negroes. Reconstruction was as yet only a word and not a procedure, although the idea of it was sufficiently resented. I remember one sign in a shop window in Richmond which read:

"What I is, I am—I won't be reconstructed—And I don't care a damn."

It brought the proprietor a number of customers, of whom, I will admit, I was one. I told him I was a Yankee.

"Oh, you a Yankee? If they were all like you I would not have the sign up."

This motto afterward became something of a slogan. During that first trip I got a very fair assortment of orders, mostly on a credit basis, the terms frequently being one half to be paid in the next fall and the other half in the fall after that. And I may say that I lost very little on this business. Those planters and merchants who could not pay when their notes became due renewed, but eventually practically all of them paid.

On my next trip through the South, a year or two later, conditions had changed for the worse and the "carpet-baggers" were in complete control in many sections. These men must have been blood brothers to the members of the rascally contractor rings, for they showed the same evidence of having none of the attributes commonly thought to be necessary in a human being. Sometimes they held offices but more often they had Negroes in the political offices and they managed the Negroes, very few of whom could read or write and who, though as a rule honest in intention, were so puffed up with power that they let the rascals do quite what they liked.

For instance, in Augusta, Ga., they levied a special tax and the carpet-bagger bosses divided up the whole proceeds. Several instances were brought to my attention where this scheme was worked. The reconstruction of the South was seriously delayed by such methods. Reputable people were not in office, because they could not take the "iron-clad" oath of allegiance, which required their testifying they had never taken up arms against the Government. The conditions were really intolerable, but what made them harder to bear was that the North received most of its reports at second hand through fanatics who were revengefully intent upon punishing the South. It was during this time that the real bitterness between North and South began; before this time only the women and a few men here and there felt very strongly or had anything approaching hate; but now, with the war over, the shocking injustice of the methods of government, all of which were laid at the feet of the North, made the feeling acute. Of course, the difficulty primarily was that the South was unable to take the oath of allegiance. Their pride stood in the way. The regular government failing to function and the people being exposed to every adventurer, they, after a time, took the law into their own hands and organized the Ku Klux Klan, an outlaw, masked, night-riding organization, but in reality a vigilance committee—the only apparent method of ensuring that justice was done and that politicians did not steal under the guise of the law.

Like all secret, irresponsible bodies, in some cases it did harm but, on the other hand, it also did much to check certain kinds of rascality. The Federal Government vigorously hunted down and punished the members, since any extra-legal government was regarded as quite out of the question. But the Ku Klux Klan numbered many worthy men who saw no other way of bettering conditions. Take the case of Colonel Ellison S. Keitt of Newberry, S. C. I had known him before the war in both a business and social way. He telegraphed me from Washington to meet him there. As soon as I had shaken hands, he said:

"I want you to go with me to see President Grant."

I asked him what was up, and he went on:

"I am supposed to be in Albany Penitentiary. I escaped arrest only because I was not at home."

He had been the head of one of the Ku Klux Klans, and his fellow members had been arrested and sentenced to the Albany Penitentiary.   I asked him if he was not afraid he would be jailed if he made himself known to the President.   He said he would take his chances; that he was at Appomattox at the time of the surrender, that General Grant had patted his horse on the head and made a remark to him to the effect that he was to take the horse home and use it on the farm; that the General seemed to take a fancy to the horse, which had a white spot on the side of its head, and that if the President did not remember him, he knew he would remember the horse.

Keitt and I gained an audience with the President.   Colonel Keitt spoke of the meeting at Appomattox and asked the President if he remembered the horse.   The President replied:

"Yes, the horse had a white patch on the side of his head."

Colonel Keitt then reminded Grant of his having been at one time the head of a vigilance committee in Indiana which ran down and sometimes hanged horse thieves.

"Now our Ku Klux has not hanged or shot anybody," said the Colonel, "but we discipline the Negroes and others who are led by an old scalawag, formerly a Negro trader, by the name of Ben Cruse. The officer in charge of the military around us is just as big a rascal as Ben Cruse, and we have to have the Ku Klux to protect our firesides.   I think you will recognize it is just as necessary for us to protect our women and children as it was to protect horses in Indiana."

General Grant at first pretended to be angry, but finally he had to laugh as he said:

"Yes, Colonel, I will grant that, but it is a bad business. If I pardon your men will you disband your Ku Klux?"

This Keitt promised to do if Grant would send some officer of good character down there and arrest Cruse. Grant answered:

"Very well, I will look into it, Colonel. In the meantime I will pardon you; as far as you are concerned you can go back with safety, and when I have investigated what you say I will take steps to remedy the situation."

Some time afterward Colonel Keitt called at my house and said he had come to thank me, that everything in his home neighbourhood was at peace, that they had sent an officer of high character down there and that Ben Cruse was arrested and in jail. I told the Colonel it was not me he should thank, but the President. He said that of course he had stopped to see the President but came on up to thank me. I took the Colonel over to a neighbour, Grier Hersh, and we talked over things connected with the war, and Mr. Hersh took us out to explain the new game of golf, a course for which he had just started. It was the first golf course started in York, and the first time it had come to my attention.

The golf course was in a beautiful field in the rear of Mr. Hersh's house, with nine holes, and various bunkers erected. When I first saw the game I regarded the idea of rational men leaving their businesss and walking over a field to hit a ball with a stick as being quite absurd, but Mr. Hersh invited me to try a round with him. Within ten minutes after we commenced I was infatuated with it, and have loved it ever since, and would recommend it to everyone who has the opportunity to play as the best possible exercise. Your troubles all vanish and you think of nothing else. I used to leave my office and drive to his golf course nearly every afternoon to play a round, and now I have a golf course on my place.

Alexander H. Stephens, after the war, took a firm stand in favour of reconstruction. He delivered an address at Atlanta while I was there. Several of our friends had told me that the South was not ready for such a speech as Stephens was certainly going to deliver, and there was going to be some fun. I had intended to go to the meeting anyway, and this decided me. His speech was eloquent and persuasive, but there were some cat calls, and when he made an eloquent defence of the fathers of the Government and the founders of our country, a man yelled out:

"You are nothing but a damned Yankee; I could eat such a little fellow as you are."

Stephens smiled and quietly remarked in his inimitable and penetrating voice:

"If you did, you would have more brains in your belly than you ever had in your head."

This created an uproarious laugh and he was not interrupted again in his speech.

I took a great interest in reconstruction of the South, and was among those who encouraged Horace Greeley to advocate shaking hands across the bloody chasm.

Governor Joe Brown of Georgia was arrested and brought to Washington, having to be brought in around from the West by way of Pittsburgh, coming down through Harrisburg on the Pennsylvania Railroad, passing through York. I took the train at York, and was introduced to him by the officer in charge, who knew me as a friend of General Thomas, who, by the way, was a resident of York during the early days of the war. Governor Brown had been at heart opposed to the separation and believed that some means should have been found to unite the country. I spoke to him of the suffering at Andersonville Prison. He replied that the accounts were not exaggerated. I must bear in mind, however, that provisions were very scarce and the feeling toward the North was bitter; but that, in spite of all, he had notified the authorities that he would open the prison gates and release the men if they could not be properly fed and cared for. We stopped off at Baltimore.

There were no through connections then. We got off at Calvert Station, and had about two hours in Baltimore before the train left for Washington. The officer in charge asked the Governor where he would like to go for dinner, and he said he preferred the Barnum Hotel, which was then at the Square, on Calvert Street near Baltimore Street. The officer said that he and his companions were going to the Eutaw House and asked Brown to join them at the Camden Station at three o'clock. The Governor went with me wholly without guard. I asked him how it was that they had arrested him and were taking him to Washington and yet he was allowed to go without guard. He said:

"I am under the strongest guard that could possibly surround me—my word of honour that I would not attempt to escape."

The North and the South did not know each other. Charles Lamb said if you know a man you cannot hate him. Had there been more intercourse between the two sections of the country there would have been no war. Some of my Southern friends directly after the war stayed with me in York *en route* north. They went as far as Boston. I begged them to visit me on returning and let me have their impressions of the North. They did. In glowing terms they said that in Boston they were treated as well as they would have been in New Orleans and Savannah—then celebrated for their hospitality and courtesy.

Once when in Savannah I went out to the cemetery, which is a beautiful place. I was feeling a little lonesome and noticed a party of young men and girls together talking. I could not resist the temptation to join them. I was received exactly as though I had known them all my life and had two or three invitations to supper at their homes.

Once I arrived in New Orleans, late of a rainy night. When I had collected my baggage at the Jackson Station the last conveyance had gone—there were no street cars. They told me at the station that they did not see anything to it but for me to stay at the station all night—there of course were no telephones and the streets were very muddy. I saw a carriage passing and hailed it. It stopped and took me and my baggage in. I remarked to the occupants—it was too dark to see who they were:

"Please let me drive you to your home and then I will have the driver take me to the St. Charles Hotel, and also have the privilege of paying for the carriage."

"The carriage happens to be my own, and I will take you to your hotel first."

She was the wife of A. T. Baldwin, the noted merchant and banker of New Orleans. I took dinner at their house by Mr. Baldwin's invitation the next night and had a very happy evening.

Business methods during this time did not greatly

change from those that had preceded the war; but a very decided change in spirit was gradually making itself manifest—the beginning of that change which is reflected in the enormous industry of the country to-day. Before the war we had been more or less content to amble on. We were in the New World but essentially we were of the Old World. Our methods were almost exactly patterned after those of England and we had not really developed a "business personality" of our own.

In this period, running from the close of the war to the Great Panic, we more than anything else developed a new outlook on business. We began to feel that business could and ought to be done in a large way; that we had to get out more goods per man; and thus the urge developed that resulted later in the invention of so much labour-saving machinery.

Many causes went toward the creation of this new atmosphere of business. First, we began to know in an intimate way that we were members of a great country. We had previously known the West—at least, we knew it was there. But I imagine that we held it more as a *hinterland* than as a part of our country—a region to go into and get things and come back from, rather than a real dwelling place. The building of railroads was changing all this and the demands for materials were so great that we simply had to visualize business on a large scale. If our population had been denser, probably we should have met the situation by employing more men. But the industrial population was really very small—we were a nation of farmers. It is probable that, scouring the country from end to end, you could have discovered few factory workmen who had not had farming experience.

My own business expanded steadily and especially in the making of threshing machines with separating attachments which the increasingly large areas that were coming under cultivation, the shortage of man power, and the introduction of the reaper raised steadily into favour. In addition we made all of our old lines—drills, cultivators, ploughs, horse mowers, and the like—and as soon as steam engines became of practical driving power for farm use, we began to make them. In farming machinery generally America was then, as now, far ahead of the rest of the world, and our commission agents, who had been unable to do any business through the war, and who discovered that, with peace, the Europeans had captured most of their old markets, found the introduction of American agricultural machinery a factor in winning their way back into foreign markets.

By the early '70's I began to have a large export trade through the commission merchants; and it was a particularly good trade because they paid cash on the docks and took over all of the credit risks. My own factory was turning out fully twice as much as before the war and that was more or less the condition through all lines of manufacture. But we were very far away from really scientific manufacture and we knew little of organization.

Always an opponent of waste, I tried to develop a cost system and did manage to keep a record of the cost of raw material and labour and I covered my overhead expense by adding 25 per cent. to the naked cost of material and labour. With all our advance in cost accounting, I find little practical improvement upon my old method. In those days, as a rule, little account was taken of overhead expense or, as the English call it, "burden." But that really was not a serious omission because the overhead charges were extremely low. For instance, I was proprietor, superintendent, foreman, office manager, cost accountant, and bookkeeper. When, later, I had foremen, they paid their own wages out of the profits from apprentices. The apprentice—and we had a great many of them—was paid only a nominal weekly amount, say $2 the first year, $2.50 the second, $3 the third, and $4 the fourth year. Many of the apprentices of that day, in their second or third year, receiving $2.50 or $3 a week, with the improved tools of to-day, could do as much as many of our skilled mechanics did then.

We did not understand anything of the possibilities of economies to be gained by increasing the overhead. It was many years later before Carnegie really revolutionized American industry by employing experimental chemists and experts and thereby accumulated an overhead that we could not at that time have comprehended. But other wastes we did avoid. We would not employ a man who did not do a full day's work. The loafer had no place in our industrial system. And also we were very careful not to waste materials. It may be that we often were wasteful of labour and held down production by trying to save materials. In a word, we practised an apparent rather than a scientific thrift.

None of us spared himself. I lived next door to the factory and did all of the office work at night and in the early morning. Of course we did not have telephone or electric power and we used the telegraph very sparingly. Kerosene torches provided light throughout most of the factory; we did have gas lights in the office and in a portion of the factory. I advertised in most of the trade journals and in the agricultural journals, but our advertisements were what to-day would be considered "cards." Also I got out what was considered a very comprehensive and well illustrated catalogue. Frequently I found, on my sales trips, farm libraries consisting of the Bible, an almanac, and Farquhar's catalogue!

Indeed, my catalogue had in it a great deal of almanac information.

Just as before the war, I was both sales manager and salesman; there was no delegation of authority. By the time that the men arrived in the morning, which was promptly at seven o'clock, I had wound up the office work and was in the factory, directing the actual work of production, helping the men wherever necessary, and hardly to be distinguished from the other workmen excepting that I wore leather gloves to protect my hands from cuts and bruises that might interfere with my office duties. And we did get our work out. I never permitted it to be said that we could not supply goods from lack of raw materials.

"The material is here," was my universal answer, pounding my desk, to any excuse as to the lack of material. By that I meant that it was my place to get the material—and I got it. It never occurred to me that the work was hard; although, as a matter of fact, I worked very much harder than any man I employed. I think that it is part of the responsibility of management for the manager to do more than any one else does. In these days of larger organization, he may have to do his more in a different way; but still he should do more. And that is not hard, for an absorbing interest takes the drudgery out of work. As Emerson says: "To the man intent upon his work, the snow is but a colour." And that applies both to the work and to the obstacles that might seem to interfere with work.

Working with the men, I knew all of them by name and if they thought that my management was too severe—though it never was—they had only to reflect that I never asked any man to do more than what I did myself. In these days I think there is too much coddling all around. I think employers and managers coddle themselves and devote far too much time to the contemplating of whether or not they are injuring themselves by overwork. And likewise, and for the same reason, there is too much coddling of employees. I do not regard ten hours as an excessive day's work and I think that ten hours of hard, interest-holding work is not as arduous or tiring as eight hours of dawdling. I have no patience at all with the prevailing precautions that managers and men take against over-work. I have always worked more than ten hours a day and find myself younger and fresher than many men of half my age who have assiduously protected themselves from over-exertion.

"Work," as Doctor Osler once said, "is the Master-Word." It has been practised by every man who has honestly succeeded. Work is the panacea and the worker is the foundation of society. The drone, organized or unorganized, is a worm that eats into this foundation, complaining bitterly as it does so. In those days all of us worked. Every man, even the sons of the rich, was expected to know a trade. As Carlyle remarked, "There are but two ways of getting a living, a man must either work or steal."

The rich man was looked up to with the deepest respect because he was thought to have gained his wealth by the possession and use of such superior personal qualities as entitled him to respect. In York, Philip A. and Samuel Small were our rich men. They had a big hardware shop with numerous side lines and did vastly more business than any other firm in the community. They were worth well over a million, while I doubt if the next richest firm possessed a fourth of that amount. P. A. S. Franklin, president of the International Mercantile Marine Company, was named after his grandfather P. A. Small.

The respect for the rich was very deep and thorough. I well remember how indescribably shocked the people were when the town drunkard, exceedingly belligerent, announced in the public square as the most original, independent, and contemptuous declaration he could make to society in general:

"I don't care a damn for Shammy Small."

Those words read him out of any possible communication with his fellow men and marked him as some kind of a lower animal. For how could a human being hold such sentiments?

Shortly after the Civil War broke out, a group

of countrymen came solemnly into town and waited on Samuel Small to request him to proceed to Washington and stop the war! People in general could not conceive of anything that he could not do. The great influence of the House of Smalls in the community arose more from their high character and liberality than from their wealth, although wealth was looked upon with more respect then than it is now. Large corporations were regarded with great respect and he was a very bold person who undertook to oppose them. For instance, one day the railroad—and the railroad was at that time an uncommonly arbitrary institution —capriciously refused to deliver coal, for much the same reason that the Negro floor manager every little while clapped his hands and stopped the dance for a few minutes—that is, just to show that he had the authority to do it. I spoke to one of the Smalls about what the railroad was doing and he replied gravely:

"It is a very dangerous thing to fight a fellow much bigger than yourself."

I replied:

"It depends on whether or not you are on the right side."

I have never found that size is of moment in a business dispute, provided that you have the confidence of being in the right. Some of the rich people on account of all the homage became acutely purse proud. It was hard for them to be otherwise.

But the Smalls never allowed their wealth to get the better of them; they remained simple, solid men.

Like most rich merchants in those days, they were also more or less involuntary bankers. The farmers were very apt to leave money with them instead of in the bank and, since this money could be forwarded to New York and put out on interest at 7 per cent., while the legal rate in Pennsylvania was only 6 per cent., the operation of receiving money was not unprofitable. In the panic of 1873 hundreds of farmers and small business men drew their money out from the banks and gave it to the Smalls. The same thing happened to Andrew Carnegie in the panic of 1907. In fact, he had to engage a man merely to keep account of the money that was sent to him for safe keeping by people that he did not know and had never heard of.

Business went forward rapidly; so rapidly that everyone began to talk of the marvellous prosperity and became a little conceited about it. And they wondered whether the years to come would bring forth the inventions and the numerous progresses of the years that had passed. We lived buoyantly and only a very few gave much thought as to what we were really living on or whether the foundations of our prosperity were planted in sand or on rock. The panic of 1873 answered that question.

CHAPTER VII

ASIDE FROM BUSINESS

THE biggest, fullest life of our family—no matter what we might do—was always in the home. My earliest and fondest recollections are of Mother and Father, who were the embodiment of kindness and solicitude for the welfare of their children, who devoted themselves to our training, and who made a home to which, when grown, we delighted to return. Both our duties and our recreations were given careful oversight, and mental training received more than the ordinary attention. Books were our daily companions and have continued during the whole of my life, to be my greatest single pleasure. My father's injunction when I left home, never to love a dollar better than a book, has been faithfully heeded—but not consciously so, because I needed no such admonition. He and my mother planted within their children a love of knowledge and of reading that has never deserted a single one of them. My father was a man of learning, interested in intellectual pursuits, a companion and exemplar to his children, while my mother was in every way a fitting helpmeet. Their attachment commenced with my mother's teaching my father French in their young days. He was then a Latin and Greek scholar, but had paid little attention to French. Under my mother's instructions he learned rapidly, and probably he needed no urging from outside to attend the sessions!

While, as was the case with many young country lads of that day, as it is of this, my youthful ambitions could see little opportunity for making progress in the limited scope of rural environment, I did not leave home without considerable reluctance and much heartburning. It meant the breaking of the tender ties which bound me to the loved place where Mother was, and I knew, and she knew, that, once they were thus so definitely broken, home could never be quite the same again. It would continue to be, so long as my mother and father were there, a place to which one would love to return, but I knew it could be so but for a brief sojourn and the sense of permanence was gone. When the children grow up and leave the home nest is one of the distressing experiences of life —an experience that I have now gone through myself. For the young it is but a temporary sorrow—for the old or ageing a poignant grief, to be concealed under a cheerful exterior for the child's sake, but none the less real and lasting.

After I came to York I wrote to my parents regularly and visited them as frequently as I could find opportunity, but I have felt regret that I did not write more often to my mother. It is the common experience to feel, when the voice that we loved is still and the spirit that we knew is no more of this earth, that we should, for our sakes and theirs, have been more attentive, more affectionate. However, my brothers and sister were still at home, and none of us were widely separated, although York then was much farther away from Sandy Spring in point of time than it is now. Since acquiring the old homestead of my great-grandfather in the community of Sandy Spring, I have frequently made the trip by automobile in three hours or less over the improved roads of to-day, but in the old days, by horse and buggy on the rough roads of the period, it would take me two days.

As previously I mentioned, my introduction to York was made easier through my family's acquaintance with Mr. Edward Jessop, who in 1856 was a partner in a hardware firm in Baltimore. It had been arranged that I should meet Mr. Jessop in Baltimore and go with him to York, where he had a country home which he visited every Friday night, returning Monday morning.

The journey from Baltimore would be considered tedious and slow in this day of rapid trips, but to me it was full of interest. Travelling on a train was a wonderful adventure. I have always enjoyed railway journeys, and I find that even to-day after hundreds of thousands of miles of it, riding on a train is a rest to me.

We reached York near midnight on the 4th of April, 1856, going from the depot to the home of Edward Jessop's father, Jonathan Jessop, then retired, who lived in York, having sold his country place, about two miles outside the town, to his son Edward. Jonathan Jessop, by the way, had been much interested in the propagation of fruits. He had a nursery on the country place, and was the discoverer and developer of the York Imperial Apple, celebrated for its excellent keeping qualities and fine flavour when permitted fully to ripen during the winter. About a year ago a stone with a tablet bearing an inscription relating this incident was erected on the farm, the unveiling being attended by officials of the state and citizens of this and other counties and states interested in fruit culture.

Saturday morning early, a conveyance from the Jessop home called for us, and we drove out to the place, which I thought very attractive with its abundance of fruit and shade trees and ornamental shrubbery. The warmth of my reception was most grateful to a rather homesick boy. Here I got the first glimpse of my future wife, who impressed me more than any one I had ever met. There were ten children in their family—four girls: Elizabeth, Hannah, Caroline, and Jeanette; and six boys: Charles, William, Jonathan, Samuel, Francis, and

Alfred. It was a bright and lively gathering as we sat down to breakfast that Saturday morning, serving to drive away any feeling of homesickness. It was taken for granted that I should stay with them over Sunday, or at least until Sunday evening, when I should have to go to town in order to be ready to start at my work early the following morning.

The time at the Jessop home passed very quickly and very pleasantly. My employer and future partner in the business, William Dingee, had been invited out on Sunday to spend the day so that we might become acquainted. There were newspapers, magazines, and an abundance of other reading matter. Edward Jessop, my future father-in-law, was an intellectual man, president of a coal company as well as of a hardware establishment in Baltimore, and was considered an authority on mining engineering. I was treated just as a member of the family, and was invited to come out Saturday evenings and spend my Sundays with them, a custom which I readily fell into and kept up until the time of my marriage, four years later. The family were musical, and after returning from the Friends' Meeting in York (Edward Jessop was a member of the Friends) we spent the time with music and in reading and conversation. As was the case at my own home, a good deal of attention was paid to the education of the children of the household. They were given tasks which would occupy a portion of the day, and had a teacher or governess. Elizabeth Jessop almost immediately engaged my attention and regard. She struck me as the most attractive girl I had ever seen, with wonderful eyes, and a mass of beautiful black curls. She was full of life, and like myself a lover of music, books, and reading. She had a lovely voice.

Edward Jessop had found me a boarding place in an attractive portion of the town on the main street not far from the place at which I was to work, at the home of a Mrs. Immel, a widow, where I was received very much as one of the family. I remained there until my marriage. I had a comfortable and attractive room looking out on the street, for which I paid $2.50 a week, including board, washing, and mending. I got Mrs. Immel's consent to erect a little observatory on the roof, the stairway to the roof being just outside my room, and there I continued my astronomical studies. I was busy in making a chart of the heavens when I came to York—I have always been greatly interested in astronomy and I knew the constellations and all the principal stars by name. Then, too, their places being unchanged, they served as a sort of link with the home folks. I knew they would be looking at the same stars.

I was on friendly terms with the workmen in the shop. I began in the woodworking department. The amount paid was nominal. I remember it was a quarter of a dollar a day for the first year, and it was proposed to advance it to 33⅓ cents the second year, but as I was made assistant manager after a year's experience, they gave me $3 a week for the second year, which was an unusual sum to pay an apprentice in those days. Then I became self-supporting—and have been so ever since. During this period I tried all sorts of experiments in diet, sometimes eating no meat, then trying but two meals a day, in an endeavour to find out what was best for me. I have since concluded that the best diet is the diet one likes best!

In looking back on those days and comparing with to-day, they seem to have been most democratic and simple. I made up my mind that, while being friendly with everyone, I should not be hasty in making close friends until I knew the people. It happened that the first house I entered in the town, aside from that of Grandfather Jessop, was that of Philip A. Small. It was my habit in the evening to bathe, dress, and take a walk up street before starting in with my books, and I thus met Mr. Small in the street. As already mentioned, he was one of York's leading citizens. Seeing me, he addressed me by name, somewhat to my surprise. I asked him how he knew me. Of course, everyone knew him. He said that he had dined with a cousin of mine in Baltimore the evening before, who had inquired about me, and he was glad to be able to tell him that I was doing

well and had already attracted notice as a stu-
dious young fellow interested in astronomy.

Mr. Small invited me to stop in and see the
family. One of his daughters, a lovely girl, was
the most intimate friend of my future wife, which
made the introduction all the more agreeable. The
youngest daughter, afterward the mother of P. A. S.
Franklin, now the head of the International Mercantile Marine Company, was then a girl in short
dresses. She was reading in a magazine an article
that set up the natural perversity of inanimate
things. I entered into an argument with her. I
urged that Nature was not cruel but kind, and
that there was no perversity. We then had a little
talk on phrenology, a science in which I had always
been interested. Some time afterward she asked
me to examine her head and write out a chart of
her character, which I did. I told her I would
have to rumple up her hair very much, and so we
went upstairs and while I was busy examining her
head and taking notes, one of the sisters came in and
exclaimed:

"Why, what in the world are you doing!"

"Simply trying to find out what sort of man she
ought to marry!" I replied.

Young people in those days were much more
sociable than they are now, or at least there seemed
to be more real friendliness in the relations. While
to-day there may be more social activity, it seems
to me to be of a hectic nature with few real attach-

ments. In the days of my youth we were closer together. Dancing was one of the diversions then as it is now, but the vulgar dances now practised in certain places were unknown. Social clubs, at which there were lively discussions of literary topics, were popular. I was president of the Addison Society, one of these. Our holidays were occupied with simple diversions, often outdoors. On the Fourth of July a band of music would be engaged and the people would go off on a picnic to some grove in the neighbourhood; patriotic addresses would be made, the Declaration of Independence and Washington's Farewell Address would be read, and the families would gather together with their friends for a picnic lunch on the ground. We would find a dance floor in a neighbouring barn—York County was famous for the size of its barns—and the young people, and often many of the older ones, would join in a Virginia reel, ladies' chain, polka, schottische, or mazurka.

It was the custom in those days to devote New Year's Day to calls. Every man was expected to stop work at noon and call on his friends in the afternoon. I got so used to doing this that I have continued it ever since, although the custom is now no longer practised. On New Year's Day of last year, or rather the first day of the present year, I decided to call on the newly installed pastor of one of our prominent churches. I had not met him nor he me, but many of his new friends and parishioners were my friends.   When I rang the bell he came to the door and very cordially invited me in and we sat by the open fire chatting for some time. After a little while he said:

"Oh, I know you now.   You are Mr. Farquhar."

We had a very pleasant little visit together. Some days afterward the Pastor's wife met me on the street.   She told me she had heard about the call, but that New Year's calls should always be on the ladies.   I told her that I had asked for her but she was not at home, and that I had a very enjoyable chat with her husband, but I promised to call on her, which I did, and found her equally attractive.

It was early in the spring of 1860 that I became engaged to be married to Elizabeth Jessop.   I had never faltered in my devotion from the first glimpse I had of her when her father took me to his home, and I was a proud and happy man when I found that my regard was returned.   We fixed upon the early autumn as the time for our marriage, which took place on the 26th of September at her home. The beautiful Quaker marriage ceremony was used: "In the presence of the Lord and before these Friends, I take Elizabeth N. Jessop to be my wife, promising with Divine assistance to be unto her a faithful and loving husband until death shall separate us."   This was repeated by both of us, and the certificate signed by all those present.

Upon our return from our wedding journey—a trip to Niagara Falls—we started housekeeping in a house which I had rented about half a block up the street from our present office. As an example of the rents of that day—I paid for the house, which was new and commodious, just $84 a year. Of course there were rumours of impending trouble between the North and the South, and there was some doubt expressed by our parents and friends of the wisdom of marrying just at that time, but we were ready to take the risk. The war clouds darkened very rapidly, and war came on apace, breaking out shortly after the election of President Lincoln. The depression in business which immediately followed caused us some anxiety, but as we were young and sanguine, of cheerful disposition, had plenty of clothes, coal in the cellar, and an ample supply of provisions, we lived very cheaply. My wife cooked the meals and I attended to the fires in the morning. My wife's mother had been careful to give her thorough training in the very useful art of cookery and the care of the household. It seems to me that this is one of the essentials in the training of girls. One hears much of the struggles of many young wives in making palatable food, leading often to extravagance in living, out of tin cans purchased at the corner grocery, thus putting a strain upon the good nature of the young husband. As the man is presumed to be fitted to make the living, so also should the wife be presumed to know how to care for the house—unless, perhaps, the girl has been occupied in some daily task outside the home, in which case there is some excuse. However, there were few young ladies in my early days who were unable to cook a meal and properly care for the home as well as make their own clothes.

Two or three years after our marriage, when business improved, I decided to build a home of my own, and the house which now contains my offices was built. We lived here from 1864 to 1874. The shop was but a step from the house, and I was so intensely occupied that most of the management of the household fell upon my wife. Here our children were born—my oldest son, William E.; our only daughter Estelle, whose death I have never ceased to mourn; Herbert, another boy who died in infancy—a beautiful child; Percival, and Francis. After the death of the children my wife's health broke down, and I had a specialist come on from the city. The local doctors told me she was not going to live, that her heart was affected and that there were other troubles. Even the specialist gave me little encouragement, but said she would live longer in some cheerful place in the country where she could get plenty of fresh air.

I went out and bought a piece of ground. I had thought of living in a tent for a while, as it was summer time, but I concluded to put up a small board house. This was completed in two days;

the third day we went out there. We lived there until early in September, and my wife's health commenced to improve right away. We had thought of going back to our house in town and building in the spring, but my wife was afraid that she would lose what she had gained and so we took rooms in a house in the country. On the 10th of September of that year I started my present house on a high hill; by Christmas we were living in it. This was in 1874, when everything was very cheap—walnut $25 per thousand feet; clean heart, yellow pine, $16 a thousand; and oak, $13. The wood used in that house did not average more than $16 per thousand feet. The house was built of the first grade of material, but at a cost of less than one quarter of what it would take to-day.

My time was so fully taken up with my work at the office and factory that there was little left to devote to my children. I have since much regretted this. I had an idea that the children would find plenty to do with the books and other interests provided for them. But these things do not take the place of intimate companionship, and I would advise all parents to make companions of their children as much as possible. It used to be my habit to go over to the factory at five o'clock in the morning, stay there till six, then go back for breakfast, returning to the factory and spending the entire day there until six, eat my supper and then at half past six go over to my office and work for several hours. Thus the training of our young children largely devolved upon my wife, and while a more excellent guide could not have been found, I must in truth admit that it was a great mistake on my part not to have given them more personal attention in their infancy. Children are one's most important asset. Whatever the children may have missed from a closer companionship, I know that I lost more. I have always been a lover of children and have never had any difficulty in attracting them to me and making them my friends. Of course, I took an interest in their lessons, helped them when I could find the time, and we always had some time together on Sundays. My boys, however, were good boys, and beyond boyish pranks and scrapes we had no special trouble with them. My oldest son, after graduating at the York Collegiate Institute, desired to enter business. The other two, however, Percival and Francis, after graduating at the Institute, went to the Sheffield Scientific School of Yale. Percival, although prepared for college, was too young, and spent two years in my office before he could enter the University. When I accompanied him for his entrance examination, there was considerable doubt expressed as to his ability to pass the examination, especially as he had been out of school for two years and had not had any special coaching. We were invited to the home of the professor in charge, however, at which we met the president of the

College, and after some conversation with my son they admitted that he was fully equal to the task.

Percival was not content to remain at home, desiring larger fields. He always had ambitious ideas. After leaving college he studied law with Dos Passos and Judge Field, and was admitted to the bar. He entered politics and was elected to the New York Legislature. In the meantime he had become associated with me as a partner in my business in New York, from which he drifted into financial operations of larger scope, his activities in this direction leading him to Cuba, South America, and Europe.

My youngest son, Francis, also studied law and went into practice in New York City. One evening at home, some years later, I remarked to my wife that I had worked mighty hard to build up the business, and as Will, my oldest son, wished to leave York and engage in constructive work, I did not believe he would want to settle down and take charge of it. The only alternative that I could think of was Frank. Frank was settled, just about to be married, and I did not think he would find New York a good place to bring up a family. My wife laughed at the idea, but I wrote Frank that night. His reply was that he owed everything material he had in the world to me and had great confidence in my judgment; that if I thought best, he was ready to come down and join me. I replied that I would put up a cottage

on my place and give him the land.   He agreed,
wound up his law business, and came on.   The
factory is now practically solely in his charge, although I keep a supervisory eye upon it and, when
called upon, act as adviser.

CHAPTER VIII

THE PANIC OF 1873

A FEW minutes before noon on September 18th, 1873, the message came over the wire to York:

"Jay Cooke & Company have suspended."

Only those who were in business then can have an idea of what that news meant to us in York and to every citizen in the nation. Jay Cooke, as the man who had financed the Civil War, had become the foremost financier of the country; to the people in general who knew nothing of finance, he was almost the financial father. That his firm could fail was all but unthinkable; as the Philadelphia *Inquirer* put it, no one could have been more surprised "if snow had fallen amid the sunshine of a summer noon." A policeman arrested a newsboy in Philadelphia for crying "All about Jay Cooke's Failure"—he could not imagine the fact of failure and thought the boy had gone mad.

The 18th fell on Thursday; by Friday morning nearly everyone with a bank account was outside his bank's doors foaming at the mouth for his deposit. No one thought of doing business. York

145

was more excited than when the Confederate Army was approaching. Every bank in town was in the midst of a run; the same condition extended over the whole country. By Saturday nearly all the banks, the private bankers, and the New York Stock Exchange had closed. President Grant was in New York trying to find some way to stop the panic.

The farmers who had entrusted their money to P. A. & S. Small stormed the hardware shop to get back what they had given to them. No man wanted to listen to reason; the bottom had fallen out of the country and the only thing in the world that counted was hard money. A currency panic is not pretty; it is a mad, unseeing, unthinking scramble for money—I saw hundreds fighting tooth and nail to get into banks—fighting as cowards fight their way out of a burning theatre. It was a terrible orgy of crude greed when a gold dollar ranked above every sentiment that makes life worth while. Personally I was not frightened; it was a shock, of course—a tremendous shock—but it has never been my habit to let my emotions run away with my sense, and anyhow it was not in my nature to rush about as though the world were going to end, just because I was threatened with the loss of a few dollars. We had been taught at home that dollars were not so valuable as all that.

So I just closed the shop and walked about to see what was going on. I would not have closed the

shop had the workmen shown up, but my workmen and all other workmen, although few of them
had any money except what was in their pockets,
were out in what might be called a sympathetic
panic!

I looked in on Philip and Samuel Small to see
how they were making out. I found them calm
and careful as ever in the offices of their store and
ready to meet all comers. Their bearing was in
no way different from usual, and the crowd of
excited farmers and townspeople that jammed
every inch of the open space and extended out into
the street might have been customers clamouring
to buy, for all the effect it had on the Smalls. They
were of that sturdy, canny, old American stock that
was equally unafraid of work or of trouble. But,
as usual, they were ready; back of them were ranged
neat piles of gold and greenbacks, and still farther
back in the shadow lay a great open sack out of the
mouth of which overflowed on to the counter what
looked like a stream of gold coins that they evidently had not had the time to stack. They were
not seeking any excuses or promising to pay
"to-morrow" or any other day. They were ready
to pay everyone, and as each depositor presented
himself, they looked up his account, calculated
the interest, and counted out the money, always
remarking as they did so, something to this effect:

"We are very glad to give you back your money
but you must understand that you are never to

come into this store again to ask us to care for your money."

To be ostracized by the Smalls meant something; to many it meant more than gold—and the gold was there for the asking. So two streams of people shoved their way out back through the crowd. The one with their money in hand, the other satisfied that their money was safe. In a couple of hours the crowd was satisfied that the Smalls were sound, and the same emotion that had begun the panic now vented itself in loud hurrahs for the Smalls.

When the store cleared, the Smalls started gathering their money to put it into the safe, and as they swept the overflow back into the great bag, one of them, with a half smile, tossed a coin to me:

"Keep that as a remembrance," he said.

It was a big bright penny! The moment they had heard of the failure the day before, Philip Small had gone to the Philadelphia mint and drawn a newly minted stock of big copper pennies! The real gold they had piled in plain sight. The "copper" gold had lurked more discreetly in the shadow. Samuel and Philip Small had stood out there as bravely and as unconcerned as though every copper penny had been a gold eagle. Of course, they were solvent—they were the richest men thereabouts—but equally, of course, they did not have all their wealth in currency.

The panic of 1873, as most people will to-day

admit, was preventable. A severe depression following a period of over-expansion was inevitable, but the panic itself had no reason for being and would not have taken place had it not been for nervousness on the part of Jay Cooke's New York partners who closed the New York branch office of the firm (the main office being in Philadelphia) wholly on their own initiative and without consulting the founder and head.

In the higher financial circles there had been a long period of nervousness. The money market was in the hands of speculators and almost any day they, like Jay Gould or Jim Fisk, could get up a corner in money. It may be remembered that the speculators almost brought about a panic on the Black Friday of 1869 by their attempt to corner gold. At the same time the currency of the country was very unsettled. Every little while someone came forward with a proposal to redeem the war bonds in greenbacks. The Franco-Prussian War, the Chicago fire of 1871, and the big Boston fire of 1872, were all unsettling influences. With money in this nervous condition, great constructive enterprises were going forward; the Southern and the Pacific Railways were reaching out, and Jay Cooke had become heavily involved in and was practically carrying the Northern Pacific. Our bankers for the first time had learned to tap Europe, and they obtained a flow of funds, at times great, but always uncertain, from abroad—from

England, Holland, Germany, and France. Members of Congress speculated freely, and subsequent investigations disclosed that a very large number of rather eminent politicians had speculative bond and stock accounts carried for them by bankers, without putting up a penny. A skilled financier would have known that the condition was dangerous, but we, in York, knew little of finance and neither did people in general throughout the country.

They saw only the prosperity, the railways being built, and above all they saw Jay Cooke as the banker of the people. He was, I think, the first to sell bonds by great campaigns of advertising in which the services of practically all the newspapers in the country were enlisted. In those days certain kinds of advertising were not distinguishable from reading matter and an advertising campaign of bonds meant the publication of article after article which were by the laity read and accepted as the matured judgment of the newspaper. Cooke had sold the war bonds in this fashion. He sold Northern Pacific bonds after the same manner. The people believed in him; they would buy anything he offered and, considering the wealth of the country, in large amounts.

The railroad bonds were pledged as collateral with banks all over the country. The whole credit structure rested on them. There was no mutuality among either banks or bankers. They might join in a profit but never in a loss—each man was out for himself and it was no one's concern that the failure of a solvent bank or banking house might temporarily ruin the country. The New York financiers could have saved Cooke and could have saved the banks, but they were intensely jealous of Cooke. They let him fail—and then failed themselves. They were jealous of one another and nobody was big enough to do as Mr. Morgan did in 1907, when he called the most powerful financial interests of the country to his library and cut off a rising young panic at the very outset of its career.

These warnings, these rumblings under the financial crust, had not been heard by any of us. Business men talked as business men always talk in times of prosperity. They could not see any end to the development of the country. In that they were right, for there can be no end to the development of this country. I have been working in it for more than seventy years and it is a very different country to-day from the day on which I started. But as compared with what is now to be done there is really more before us than there was at the time of the Civil War—because we now know how to utilize more resources.

In January, 1873, J. L. Mott, the president of the Iron and Steel Association, said before its New York meeting that the country would never see pig iron selling below its then price of $40 a ton—that it could never get below that price but that it would go higher. That prediction made a great impression on the country, for Mott was an authority. Within the year pig iron dropped to $18 and $20 and at one time it was offered at $13— practically without takers! Jones, of Jones & Laughlin, the big steel producers, made the same sort of prediction, and everywhere we heard detailed prophecies showing exactly why high prices and prosperity were with us for ever. If any one suggested that perhaps the prices of the future were in the laps of the gods and not in the minds of men, he was promptly squelched as a calamity howler!

At the next meeting of the Iron and Steel Association following the panic, at which Mott appeared on the platform, he was hissed by some of those who had taken his advice. He got up and said:

"My speech will be very short: If my foresight were as good as my hindsight I should be better off by a damned sight."

This elicited a laugh, put them all in good humour, and as I remember he was reëlected.

The abundance of predictions that never again should we see low prices, that the country's needs were infinite, and that the best we could hope to do was to keep within hailing distance of demand, really prevented much progress in truly economical business. People were too busy to think of economy. They were not, as I have previously remarked, so skilled in extravagance as we are to-day, but considering their lights they did what they could. Many sellers showed a disposition to consider the buyer as a poor beggar without the gates, to whom anything might be thrown! We had the seller triumphant and the buyer despondent. The successive supremacies of buyers and sellers give a most amusing business panorama. As demand exceeds supply, so does a crown of arrogance grow on the head of the seller, but the moment the tide turns, the buyer takes over this crown, full-grown, and then no slave to an oriental potentate ever had to go through such elaborate abasement as the newly crowned buyer requires of the seller. I find, looking back through all these years, that the men who, as buyers or sellers, keep level heads and do not force their transient advantages, in the long run reap the real profits. The man who cannot stand prosperity is also useless in adversity. In good times he is out in the street making a nuisance of himself; in bad times he is slinking through the halls of the bankruptcy courts.

The blow of the panic was so sudden, so swift, and so tremendous, that it left the country literally paralyzed. Those who had been shouting prosperity began dolefully to whine that the country was done for, that it was dead for ever and a day, that there was no use trying to do anything because there was nothing to do. For a hundred days this coma lasted. The Christmas of 1873 was about as cheerless a festival as has ever been intoned.

Having an eye for the brighter side and an abounding faith in the righteousness of God and the essential integrity of man, I could not share in the hopelessness about me. My shop stayed shut for exactly four days. I opened again on the Monday following the panic and I should have opened earlier had not my men been disorganized.

I was doing a good export business, and it occurred to me that the whole world was not involved in the panic, that there certainly must be customers to be found somewhere. I went on to New York, visited the commission merchants, and asked them whether business could not be had. They said it could always be had at a price. After going over the situation thoroughly I solicited and secured a lot of orders, optional to accept or reject within a week, at an average of 25 per cent. under the prevailing prices. The next thing was to see if I could fill them.

I went back to York, called all my employees together, and explained the condition of things. I told them I could start up if I paid them on the basis of a 25 per cent. reduction in their wages, but if at the end of six months the conditions warranted it and if wages in general had not come down sufficiently to cover the decreased margin, I would pay them the difference. I asked them to think over the proposal and let me know. They did not want to stop work. Some of them voted at once to accept, others said that within six months things would be as good as ever, and they would get the difference anyhow. But one single man in the factory declined to accept the terms I offered. He left, and after several weeks came back, saying he could find no work anywhere and would go to work at half price, but I took him back, of course, on the same terms with the rest. They were all very fair and none had the spirit of holding up that is now so prevalent. They had the elemental sense to see that without work they could not live. The bearers of nostrums that will permit life without work were not then among us.

With the labour side settled, I went out after raw materials. I wrote to the dealers, asking them if they would sell me goods payable one half cash or its equivalent, notes with interest, the balance payable at the end of six months. The final price of the goods was not to be settled until the end of the six months' period when we would take the then ruling market price and adjust the differences. This seemed fair to me, for with the panic on, no one knew what prices would obtain. Some of them asked if I took them for damned fools, but enough of them accepted my offer to supply me with goods, and I may say that at the end of six months I had very little extra to pay them. I got a good deal at half price, and nothing at more than three fourths the price prevailing before the panic. At the end of six months prices had dropped to such an extent that I was required to make an extra payment in only a few instances and in none over 75 per cent. of the former price, hence my 25 per cent. reduction in price of my goods was fully covered and wages had fallen so low that not a single workman asked for or expected an advance on what I was paying.

With both my labour and materials at a quarter below the market I was able to go ahead while others were standing still. But I needed ready cash; I had to pay cash for wages and the purveyors of a few essential supplies would take nothing but cash for their wares. One of the several causes for the long duration of the panic was the breakdown of every kind of credit; we cannot do business without credit, and whenever any considerable number of men in business or banking become so frightened that they will not extend credit, then business ceases. Business is founded on confidence; when confidence is withdrawn as a general commodity, then business itself must topple and fall. Whenever the so-called "hard-headed," cash-fondling business man obtains a majority in public opinion, then credit stops and business ceases. The man who never extends credit is a greater menace than the man who extends credit too freely.

The bank with which I had been doing business in York joined in the craze for cash. The bank's officers notified me that they would no longer give me credit or discount customers' notes. How they expected to make money by keeping their funds in the vault is one of the several things I have never been able to fathom. I imagine that their logic did not extend so far. Panics do not teach logic. I asked them how about customers' notes which they had already discounted. A good many of them would have to be renewed. That was certain. The bank officers said they would not renew, that they would have to look after the interests of their other customers. I have never discovered why they took this stand against me unless it was because they were afraid of my recklessness in starting up business so quickly.

The whole Board of Directors, however, was not against me. Latimer Small and Daniel Rupp both stood by me, remarking that I had always been a good customer, and prompt in my payments. Latimer Small made it a personal issue and resigned from the Board. He declared that he would see that my needs were cared for and that his father would come down to see me. His father, Philip Small, was president of the York County Bank. He did come down, went all over my factory, and my books from end to end, and then said:

"It is all right; the York County Bank will take care of you, you can bring your accounts up to us."

And so I managed my credit and I made money. But it was hard, grinding work. Mine was the only factory in town that, day in and day out, after the worst days of the panic were over, managed to keep going full-handed. For there was no sudden pick-up after this panic. The gold standard had not been restored, the country was financially unsound, and the money was not coming into the land from Europe. The overseas investors had been thoroughly scared off—as well they might have been. People at home were afraid either to buy or did not have the money. I got most of my business on long credits—one- and two-year paper that I had to carry with the bank. I remember one man who wrote down from Somerset County, Pennsylvania, asking for a saw-mill engine and equipment. He wrote me word he wanted to pay by a note. I told him I could not furnish the goods unless the note was exceptionally good. He replied that it was, sending a testimonial from the presiding judge of the county and a bank that the note he proposed to give was absolutely good. When it came, to my amazement it was for nine years. It looked to me like a trick. I wrote him that I could not accept it, and then I found that his desire for nine years' credit was due to the fact, which he had not disclosed, that he would come into a large fortune in nine years. His local bank agreed to take up the note just as soon as they found what he was doing and I received the cash.

I made money. I have always made money in panics. Those who would not give credit or could not finance credits did not make money, and everywhere were unemployment and stark destitution. A workingman would work for almost nothing; I did not unfairly lower the wages of my men; they did honest work and were entitled to honest pay, and that they got. But in other parts of the country were riots and bloodshed. The railroad men along the lines of the Pennsylvania started open warfare; they burned the shops at Columbia and Harrisburg near by and for a time all traffic stopped. The workers were desperate and willing to follow any one; the proprietors were equally desperate and saw nothing ahead. And everyone in the most irritating way did his saving at the spigot and then let the bunghole flow copiously. The country tried to do business with self pity as its only disclosed asset.

I had no self pity. It is a recreation that I have always denied to myself. But I might have indulged myself a little, for in 1876 when, after days and nights of unending labour, I was fairly on my feet, my factory and all I owned were one Sunday completely wiped out by fire. I found myself back once more at the point from which I had started years before.

As soon as I found that nothing could be done to save the plant, I got the telegraph office to open (they closed on Sundays) and sent messages to most of the various houses on which I depended for supplies, telling them that I had been burned out but would shortly start up again and wished to buy materials, which I would want at cash prices, to be settled by notes with interest. Extensions and credits were not then easy to get. There was general distrust, manufacturers and jobbers were very careful whom they trusted. In going over my books and what assets were left I calculated I was just about even with the world, just where I had started, twenty years before.

Some of the dealers wired in reply that they would continue to sell to me at cash rates, taking my notes with interest for the old account, and generally they promised to do everything they could to help me regain my footing. Fortunately, my credit was of the highest. I had followed the rule of Hamilton Fish never to break a financial promise; I always paid every note when due unless there was an understanding that it could be renewed. I remember that the commercial agencies were obliged to rate me blank as to capital but high as to credit.

My father came up from Sandy Spring and my father-in-law did not go to Baltimore on Monday. We all met to discuss the situation and decide what I could do. I had, they said, quite a nice little line of business and a good business in repairs, of course, and they thought I might start in on a small scale and probably build up again in a modest way making enough to live on while I was doing it. They were rather gloomy as to the outlook, and were in a sense justified, for it was, indeed, a heavy blow, especially as we were in the midst of a business depression, which was not over until '79. I, however, had other ideas.

I called on Michael Schall, who was the assignee of H. S. Myers & Co., who had failed and whose building was right along the railroad at no great distance from my factory. I knew if I could get hold of that shop and foundry, I could start business right off on the next morning. I asked Schall if he would sell and he said:

"Oh, yes, I will sell it to you."

He named a price, after some dickering, that was satisfactory to me. I suggested that we go to Lawyer Latimer, which we did, and drew up a bill of sale, which Schall signed, selling me the property at the price. Latimer said:

"You must make a cash payment in real estate transactions to make this binding."

I asked: "How will $5 do?" That was all I had in my pocket.

Mr. Schall was satisfied and I gave him the $5, folded up the paper, and put it in my pocket. I told him I would take possession of the property the next morning. Surprised, he exclaimed:

"You can't do that, I am winding up the business."

"But," I answered, "I must have a place to start business in, and the property is now mine."

"No," he replied, "I cannot consent to that at all. I will give it to you in thirty days."

Latimer, the Attorney, told him I was right, that I could take possession of the property, for he had sold it to me. After some heated discussion we finally arranged that he should have the privilege of finishing up his work there, but I could move in at once and commence business. He then asked:

"When do you expect to pay for it?"

I replied: "I haven't the remotest idea in the world; I will pay you as fast as I can make the money."

"That I won't stand for," he declared, point blank.

Latimer remarked: "You can't help yourself. The court would assume, in case you brought suit, that it was to be settled for in a year and it might take another year to get the money."

Schall said: "Well, I guess I am in for it."

Latimer advised against any legal action, told him he thought he had done the best he could for the Myers creditors, and we all let the matter rest as it was and the transaction closed with a laugh all round. I made my arrangements to start up on the next morning. But that was not all; I also got under way plans for further extension. I felt I must double my business as I should need half of it as a sinking fund to cover my loss.

I had a talk with Peter McGuigan, who was a contractor, and he agreed to put up a new factory for me if I would pay about half his crew's wages as they came due—he to carry the rest until I could pay it. I also saw the Billmeyer & Small Co. and they agreed to furnish the lumber. McGuigan said he would furnish the brick.

These things settled, I returned to the office and told those who were there going over my affairs, that I had contracted for a new building to be put up, larger and more complete than the other in every respect and more nearly fireproof, and that also I had bought the property down below. They were astounded.

"How can you do all this? You can't pay. How are you going to pay?" they asked all at once.

I replied very confidently: "I have been too busy to think of that."

This made them angry and one went on:

"It is impossible; you have lost your right senses. It is crazy to think of going ahead on the scale you propose. Where will you get credit? As soon as people find you have been burned out and can't make a showing they will refuse to furnish you anything except for cash."

"On the contrary," I answered, "I will probably buy on one or two years' time at cash prices." Then I handed them the telegrams: George Small—"all the pig iron you want; pay for it when you please"; Billmeyer & Small—"You may pay for the lumber in 18 months."

Wm. F. Potts & Sons—"All the steel you want, pay for it when it suits you, cash prices, notes with interest"; Grubb, the same thing with pig iron, and so on. I bought everything on six, twelve, and eighteen months, so that I was able to manufacture the raw material, sell the goods, and get paid for them before I had to pay for all of the material. My workmen of their own accord offered to work for 15 per cent. less on their wages for thirty days while I was getting started and into shape.

When those who had gathered to hold a post mortem over my business saw how ready the outside dealers were to assist and how ready the workers were to pitch in, one of the bankers turned round and said:

"It looks to me that we who have been dealing with Mr. Farquhar right here in his home town, and always found him prompt in meeting his obligations, ought to treat him as well as people who live elsewhere. For my part, I shall advocate continuing his credit at our bank."

One by one they shook hands with me, pledged their support, and went on their ways, confident that I would work out. I did. I fulfilled every promise and met every note—and have not failed so to do from that day to this.

CHAPTER IX

THE NEW ERA OF PROSPERITY

ONE of the largest industrial figures that emerged out of the panic of 1873 was Andrew Carnegie; we did not fully recognize his genius at that time—Jones & Laughlin were among the most prominent iron and steel manufacturers—but Carnegie had already made his start before the panic broke and with his extraordinarily skilled management of finance, the panic found him in far better condition than any of his competitors. Even a strong man will not come through a panic unharmed, but as compared with weaker competitors he will be relatively stronger at the end than he was at the beginning. So it was with Carnegie.

Most of the iron men had tied themselves up in railroads, for not only did the railroads need the metal in large quantities but they afforded speculations in which fortunes might be turned over night. A man with any standing at all could borrow almost to the issue value on new railroad securities put out by prominent houses and a great number of business men took advantage of this to carry great blocks of stocks and bonds on very narrow margins.   Carnegie had bought into several roads with his friends, President Thompson and Vice-President Scott of the Pennsylvania Railroad, but, contrary to the general practice, Carnegie bought and paid for everything that he owned.   The bank panic did not touch him.

It was one of his absolute rules never to speculate and at one time he resolved never to own a share of stock or a bond that was even listed on the Stock Exchange or freely traded in.   I am not certain, but I think his only deviation from this rule was in connection with the bonds he took for his holding when selling out to the United States Steel Corporation.

My first meeting with Carnegie was in Secretary Stanton's office sometime during the Civil War.   Thomas A. Scott had been appointed Assistant Secretary of War in charge of transportation; Carnegie had been Scott's telegraph operator and assistant in the railway and had come along. He was a young man, of about 25 years, I think, not imposing in appearance and rather shy in manner, but it took only a moment or two of conversation to gain a peculiar sort of confidence in him.   Carnegie was one of those men you instinctively had to trust.   That is why I call the confidence he inspired "peculiar."   You did not stop to wonder, "Will he do?" and then answer, "Yes."   You simply decided at once, "He will do." Although Scott held the official title, it was Carnegie who did most of the work. One of his most important exploits was the building in one night of a railway bridge over an unfordable stream in front of the Union forces under General Dodge, which enabled that general to win a great victory. General Dodge afterwards told me that being able to surprise the enemy and win a battle when the Confederates thought they were safe for a week, won him promotion, but that the credit was very largely due Carnegie for his resourcefulness and skill in quickly providing the bridge.

I had many opportunities to meet with Mr. Carnegie later in life, but even at this first meeting in the few minutes I had with him I was impressed with the ease and unerring touch with which he handled men. Scott was hard to see; Carnegie, with far more detailed duties than Scott, was open to everyone. He had no waiting line outside his office; he let everyone in and then attended to them one at a time and seemingly without effort. He got what any one had to say, disposed of the matters, and sent the caller off amiable, if not satisfied, in less time than it would have taken formally to usher him in. He had Scotch caution in plenty but so quick was he to turn over every phase of a subject that one might easily think some of his decisions were at first impression when really he had simply considered every phase in a moment.

In these days it is rather the habit to jibe at the

scholar in business—the thought seems to be that a man is all the better for a lack of knowledge of *belles lettres* or of an intimacy with the masters of art and literature. Carnegie was as keen a business man as ever lived; he was keen in the large way—he saw not merely to-morrow but the day after. And one of the reasons that he so quickly got into large business was that through his study of the literary masterpieces he came to know human characteristics. For after all, great literature is only the preservation of the best thought on human nature.

Having this greater mastery, Carnegie never became lost in details—never allowed himself to take a temporary advantage of any one, or to do anything that compromised his conscience. He was too wise to be little and it may surprise many to know that this young man who was first a telegraph messenger, then an expert telegraph operator, then an expert railroad man who would probably have been president of one of our biggest systems if he had not desired to get into business for himself, and who was already a power in iron before he was thirty, entertained an ambition to get out of business as soon as possible and spend the remainder of his life in study. He wanted to go to Oxford or Cambridge and mix with literary men. His affairs, however, grew so rapidly that he could not satisfy his real ambition; but he did determine that, above all, he would not dedicate his life merely to the making of money. With all his hard common sense, great business ability and Scotch shrewdness, he was a man of ideals; he agreed with Lincoln that the object of life was to contribute your mite—whether spelled m-i-t-e or m-i-g-h-t—to being of use. I know of no one who has been of more material benefit to America, and few who have put opportunities for education and improvement in the way of so many, by the wisdom of his benefactions, than Andrew Carnegie. He conducted the largest business of his time, made the best product, sold it at the lowest price, and paid the highest wages, making America the iron and steel centre of the world.

We all know that he made a great sum of money —but he did not make it in great gains at any one time, with the exception of the release of his holdings to the new corporation that the late Mr. Morgan formed. And then he really only took in negotiable form the value of what he already had accumulated in plants, mines, and goodwill. He earned his money in a constant flow and as a student of business and of men. Management was not with him a matter of rules; he kept in close touch with the affairs of the world—he read and travelled widely. Thus he gained a perspective that enabled him usually to see what was coming and then to arrange his affairs accordingly. He believed that knowledge was power and demonstrated that fact. As a youngster he

had access to the library of Mr. Anderson of
Allegheny; he studied while others played.

I might mention a very interesting incident
connected with his introduction to this library.
While a messenger boy, he was sent over early in
the morning with a telegram to Mr. Anderson,
with instructions to wait for an answer, as it was
important.   Mr. Anderson had returned late that
night, and the butler said he could not wake him.
Young Carnegie walked into the library, took a
seat, and became immersed in a volume upon steel
making and the tremendous advantages of steel
over iron.   Mr. Anderson finally came down with
his answer to the dispatch. The lad turned,
apologizing for having taken the book.   The steel
master—Anderson was engaged in the steel business—asked if he was interested in the subject.
Carnegie said:

"Oh, yes, it is fascinating to me."

"Take the book home and read it, and return it
when you are through with it," answered Mr.
Anderson.   This he did; was told to take another,
and that he might have access to the library; and
Mr. Carnegie told me that then and there he made
up his mind if he ever became wealthy he would
found libraries and give young men the same
opportunity that had been afforded him.

The knowledge Mr. Carnegie thus attained
through reading and study he applied first to one
thing and then to another—to telegraphy, to

railroading, to iron-making. By the time the other boys had finished playing, Carnegie had almost finished working and was ready to play. He used his knowledge of men and things to direct; while in his early twenties he had already the capacity to get others to carry out his plans. He knew he had that capacity and used it, and thus apparently with ease he became a great captain of industry.

He was among the first to apply scientific brains to business—to know that results are not to be gained merely by luck. He is said to be the first man to employ chemists in analyzing products needed in iron- and steel-making. He built on what his competitors threw away. It so happened that he applied his genius to iron and steel but he could have elevated equally any industry in the country. He selected iron and steel first because they were basic and second because his railroad experience had made for him many warm friends among the users of iron and steel.

Just as he mastered the scientific process or secured those men who could, so also did he judge business conditions, and I recall a conversation I had with him some time before the '73 Panic. I asked him why he did not build more furnaces and he said rather gaily that it would be cheaper to wait and buy the plants that the other men were building. He did not, in so far as I know, foresee the big panic, but he did know that many iron masters were going ahead too furiously in their new construction.

I have always held Andrew Carnegie to be the world's greatest business man, and I think he became so because he was not a business man in the sense of knowing nothing but business. That much esteemed "hard-headed" quality in business men comes only from a lack of imagination that really prohibits the growth to the stature of "big business men."

For instance, Carnegie was, perhaps, the first to grasp the ideal business policy—a large output sold at a reasonable price that includes a fair profit, and at the same time permits good wages to workmen and high compensation to managers. He paid men as no one before him had ever paid them—he was always anxious to share. No business head has ever commanded more loyalty from his managers and men. This is the more remarkable because he moved from Pittsburgh to New York in order to be nearer finances and the centre of things. He was in the manner of being an absentee landlord, but he went out to Pittsburgh so frequently and made himself so personal a being while around the plants that all the workmen felt they knew him—whether or not they did actually. A few of his old men still persisted in calling him Andy. I asked Mr. Carnegie once:

"Do you permit that?"

"Yes, I like it," he said, smiling.

The loyalty and the attachment of his managers were marvellous. I attended one of the Ways and Means Committee sessions during Cleveland's administration. Mr. Carnegie testified that he did not need a tariff on certain manufactures. He had never relied upon tariffs; felt that he was abundantly able to manage the steel business without assistance from the Government. Later Mr. Schwab came in and testified quite to the contrary in regard to some certain sizes of steel. When the chairman told him what Mr. Carnegie had just said, instantly Mr. Schwab exclaimed:

"Did Mr. Carnegie say that? Then I will take it all back. If Mr. Carnegie said that, it is right."

Carnegie had those elements that go to make up what I call genius—that is, not so much the possession of extraordinary attainments as the power to hold on to whatever he acquired and use each accession of attainments as stepping stones to further progress.

Genius as thus defined involves concentration of effort and the elimination of unnecessary mental or physical activity. System in action and thought is essential to success. But system of itself is idle. Thought is of no use without arrangement, but neither is arrangement without thought.

I watched the progress of two factories in my line of business that started at about the same time in Illinois a number of years ago. The proprietors of each had about the same capital and apparently equal ability. The one failed and the other succeeded. The successful man, Mr. Bradley, told me his motto was: "Handle nothing twice." He systematized his business and allowed nothing to be handled twice—no article was laid down to be picked up again, but was placed on a truck and moved to the point of next operation and thence onward until it reached the place of shipment. In the other factory the work moved hither and thither, the operatives seemed busy, but a good deal of their effort was scattered—and the company went nowhere.

Carnegie was always going somewhere and by the most direct route. He conspicuously differed from the other big figures of his day in being a manager of men rather than an expert on his own account. Many men knew more about iron and steel but none knew so much about iron and steel and men and business.

A. T. Stewart, and to a degree Marshall Field, were, on the other hand, individualistic experts. They were first of all remarkable merchandisers, and Stewart, in particular, was not so much a judge of human capability. I am not sure that Field was either. My information and observation were to the effect that Mr. Higinbotham, a highly valued personal friend, really made himself a partner by sheer credit ability. When I first began to take on some business in the

Middle West I stepped into Marshall Field's to inquire concerning the credit of several of my prospective customers. It was Mr. Higinbotham, then a young man, who gave me the information I wanted and without referring to a record. In the early business days we had but little use for records; a man was expected to remember all that was worth knowing about his business.

I took pride in carrying in my head the orders I secured on even the longest trip and sometimes did not bother to list them at the factory—I could as easily have forgotten the names of my children as the names and wants of my customers. I believe that at almost any time in those earlier years I could have reconstructed my account books from memory. On one occasion when I was employing a number of men, fifty or more, I did not have the opportunity to enter the payroll before paying off but on the following Monday I had no trouble at all in making up an exact record. We lived in our business and it was no effort to remember every detail.

Marshall Field was a buyer and seller of intuitive ability: he knew what everything ought to cost and at what it could be sold as by instinct, but more than that, he knew what the public would buy. However, A. T. Stewart and not Marshall Field was the leading merchant during the period immediately following the Civil War and he was even more individual than Marshall Field—so

much so, that his business never could accommo-
date itself to another hand and travelled only on
the momentum of the founder from the time of his
death to its purchase by John Wanamaker.

Stewart, in spite of the dignity of his appearance
and the austerity of his manner, was never too old
to keep his business eye open.   To the end of his
days he retained the keen business-getting sense
that prompted him to perform one of the dodges
that attracted customers to him as a young man.
This was to have a supply of umbrellas with him
at church on wet days in order to offer them to the
ladies who might be rain bound.   The umbrellas
had the address of the store inside and the idea was
to have the ladies return them to the store and there
become interested in the merchandise.   Though
his schemes for attracting attention had become
more dignified in later years, they were quite as
effective.

Although Stewart had all these little traits and
was, indeed, a close buyer and seller who made
every dollar tell, he was also in many ways ahead
of his time.   When he built his Ninth Street store
in New York he was generally taken to be crazy
for moving so far away from the centre of the
shopping district, which was then around Grand
Street.   He had what might be called merchandising vision and an infinite capacity, but neither
he nor Field was in any sense a man-builder and
it was expertness in detail—not science—that

made them successful. Carnegie found new ways and developed a whole new theory of scientific business. That is why I class him as the greatest business man the country has ever known.

Business has, however, lost something of craftsmanship with the passing of the old expert owner who was always there and always insisted upon knowing all about everything that was done. The new way is better; it is always better to go about a task scientifically than by rule of thumb but the new way is impersonal and always encounters the danger that spurious and not real science may be adopted. They look alike. Much of that which is called "scientific" in business to-day reminds me of the old doctor who talked in a jargon that no one on earth understood, including himself—and then let some blood. No matter what set of learned phrases he employed he ended up by blood-letting and the patient recovered in inverse proportion to the amount of attention the doctor paid to him! We are tempted to experiment with business formulas that will take the place of brains applied through hard work.

Brains and hard work are still the foundation of business and are also the driving force that carries it on. No substitutes will be found.

In the old days we undoubtedly did more hard work than is necessary to-day; or, to put it another way, the same amount of hard work to-day would yield greater results. My own methods were typical of every man who tried his best to get along. I spent, after the Civil War as well as before, an average of twelve to fifteen hours a day in the shop and office—although I always managed to spend an hour or more in reading books bearing upon business matters, world affairs, and general literature, I have, in fact, never forgotten my father's injunction to love a book more than a dollar. Not a purchase could be made in the early days, not even a nail bought, without my approval. Every manifest and bill had to be submitted to me before being mailed. I was cashier; I paid all bills and I received all moneys. I wrote or dictated every letter, made every estimate of cost, and no one had the authority to close a sale without me; in fact, I did nearly all of the selling. Selling was on a somewhat different basis from that of to-day because so many of the sales were between principals and they were thus on a social basis. The buyer and seller met on equal terms. I often stayed overnight at the homes of the customers at their insistence, while we always kept open house at York for such customers as desired to come to the factory and see what we had. We did not drop business when we left our offices—the line between office and home was hazy—and since both buyer and seller had all the information they needed for any transaction right in their heads, a salesroom was any place where a man with a desire to buy met another with something to sell to him.

Travelling then was far less luxurious than it is to-day and I wish the salesmen who complain of spending so much time on sleeping cars could have been with me on some of my trips before the era of sleeping cars. On one trip I spent thirteen successive nights in day coaches. Still, one can in time learn to get a fair night's sleep by skilfully curling across two seats! Years later, when Pullman chair cars came in, we considered them far too luxurious for ordinary travel. We frequently took box lunches along—the dining car which came along years later was considered an extravagance, though we often ate at the railway restaurants where the trains stopped for meals.

I have always taken the view that the amount of work one might personally do was limited only by the hours of the day and never by arbitrary and illogical formulas such as "Eight hours for work, eight hours for sleep, and eight hours for play." One gains strength by overcoming obstacles; I took a positive interest in surmounting difficulties, in improving methods of work, and in keeping in the closest touch with my customers. And so my life, in spite of the seemingly long hours, has been very happy. The enjoyment one gets out of work is far greater than the enjoyment which is arduously cultivated for itself. I never did any physical work which was as hard as the work of a player in a baseball game, to say nothing of a game of football, nor did I ever do any mental work more difficult than many of my school problems.

I have no belief at all in the possibility of over-work. People break down not from work but from a lack of ordinary care of the person, or from a lack of a moderate amount of exercise, or from over-eating, or under-sleeping, or from a want of interest in their work. The last mentioned cause is the most important. Breakdowns in my experience arise not from the useful work that one does but from foolish pursuit of what is ironically termed "pleasure." I do not think it is possible for any one to have his health impaired by any amount of work so long as that work holds interest, and he makes a play of it. I am inclined to believe that a very considerable amount of what we to-day call "the high cost of doing business" is due to the high cost of trying to escape useful work.

The factory was as much under my personal supervision as the office. I kept a constant eye upon the amount of production not only of each department but of each man and did my utmost to avoid any sort of waste whether of material or of human labour. Every employee had to be a producer or get out. The soldiering workman had no chance at all. His fellows would have gotten rid of him had I not and sometimes I wonder whether the modern disposition of so many workers to loaf on the job, to try to get something for nothing, and to do a minimum instead of a maximum amount of work, is not an aping on their part of what they see those above them trying to do. A poor master breeds poor men.

Our foremen, for instance, were expected to supply and manage enough apprentices to pay their own salaries. They had not only to superintend the men under them but also to scout for likely boys to be apprenticed to the trade. It was not difficult to find apprentices—we always until recently had more applications than places. But then, as now, it was hard to pick out the boys of greatest promise. None of us would have bothered for a moment with the "choosy" sort of boy who seems to have grown up during wartime. It was a privilege to be allowed to learn a trade and only those who both could and would learn were tolerated.

The amount of indirect labour and of supervisory labour was at an absolute minimum—although we did not then have the separation into direct and indirect labour. We vaguely classed indirect labour in overhead. This did not cause us any difficulty, for we were small, and with every man a producer, the overhead really amounted to less than the interest upon the value of the plant and the allowance for depreciation. There is a doubt, anyway, whether plant investment is an overhead expense, and depreciation did not then amount to so much as now, for tools were not so hard pressed and new inventions were not so frequent as to make obsolescence a real factor. I have always been interested in discovering costs but I then had no cost system in the modern sense. I approximated costs by carefully following the amount of labour and material that went into a certain batch of goods and then standardizing that as an average basic cost. On the whole, however, my costs were not so far from the actual costs as shown by modern cost keeping as one might imagine. I frequently revalued the standards and later comparisons convinced me that the error in any one case was seldom as much as 10 per cent. and that the average up and down gave a net figure very close to the real costs. I uniformly added 25 per cent. as the minimum charge to the cost of labour and material to cover all overhead and profit and loss account, and on that basis I made money.

This was a rule-of-thumb method but it is remarkable how really expert one will become through long experience in "cut and try." Most people are familiar with the ability of a grocery clerk to scoop out a pound of sugar—an expert clerk will hit the weight within a fraction of an ounce. We could likewise estimate the weight or quantity of materials. I could judge with my eye the number of feet of lumber or the weight of pig iron on a railroad car. I could tell whether the amount was short or over the invoice. My estimate was rarely 5 per cent. wide of the mark. This was not a faculty peculiar to me. It was quite common for a man to be an expert judge of the quantity as well as the quality of whatever commodity he dealt in.

Of course, it took longer to do our work then than it does now. Remember that we had no stenographers or typists, and had either to write our own letters or dictate them to good penmen who transcribed as we talked. It was an easy matter to keep two men thus going and for a time I managed three men but one night my wife came in when I was dictating to three clerks and said:

"Arthur, in that way lies madness; you have got to stop it."

I had already found dictating to more than two very wearing and so I gave up trying to imitate Napoleon and limited myself to two clerks. A man to-day can in an hour dictate more to a good stenographer than we could then dictate to two longhand clerks in several hours. This may or may not be an advantage, for having what one says taken down in longhand tends to a crisp brevity of expression which is lost when rapidly talking to a stenographer.

Business then had its pleasant sides but it also had its unpleasant sides. Its morals were not as good as to-day. The leading men were as a rule scrupulously honest; many of the smaller men were not, and even in the largest and most reputa-

ble concerns it was sometimes considered quite
legitimate to get a prospective customer drunk in
order to capture his order, if it could not be obtained otherwise. In fact, drinking was quite
commonly associated with selling, and I have
heard concerns boast that they had salesmen who
could outdrink all comers—for, of course, it spoiled
the whole game if by chance the salesman got
drunk ahead of the customer. Then the tables
might be turned. A jug of whiskey was often to
be found on the sideboard, and sometimes in the
offices, and drinking was looked upon with a great
deal more leniency than in later years.

In most companies, drinking by employees was
tolerated, as long as it did not seriously interfere
with a man's duties. As business became more
strenuous, business men began to see that they
themselves, as well as their employees, must have
every faculty alert in order to meet the exacting
demands of modern trade, and that business and
strong drink cannot profitably be mixed. I managed my affairs differently. I did not mix whiskey
and business and never, through my whole business career, gave a drink in connection with any
business transaction. I did not sell the less for that
but sometimes I did have to explain. I recall that
in New York I sold a man a large order for which
he agreed to pay cash on delivery. Then I asked
him, as was the custom, to luncheon. We ordered
luncheon and then he rather broadly hinted that

it would also be a good idea to have something to
drink. I told him I did not drink myself, and had
made it a fixed rule never to order liquor in pro-
moting a sale, but I made no objection to him as
my guest ordering what he wanted.

He took it all in good part and I do not recall
ever having lost a dollar's worth of orders through
the strict rule of not having liquor form part of
any transaction.

Now those were buyers' markets—as is normal
—and the idea behind the excessive treating was
not alone good fellowship and an ingratiating attempt to gain favours, but all too often was
disguised bribery, and as a natural result there
was a good deal of out-and-out bribery concealed
under various disguises. It was a too frequent
practice to offer commissions in sales to other than
the principals—a practice so generally known to
exist that employers rather took it as a matter of
course, especially since in some cases they were
guilty of encouraging their salesmen to indulge in
this sort of thing. Since it is, of course, impossible to get the best results if one's agent evolves
an interest in opposition to that of his employer,
the truth of the old adage that honesty is the best
policy in business, as well as elsewhere, began to
dawn upon the latter. The morals of business
have decidedly improved.

During this period until 1879 business was dull.
In 1877 prices were so low that it was difficult to

make a profit. It was all that people in domestic business could do to make bare livings, and many of them did not do that. My export business furnished my principal source of profit and enabled me to go steadily ahead where those who depended solely upon inland business frequently stood still. In 1879 prices began to improve, building gradually started, payments in gold, which had been suspended since the panic, were restored, and then began slowly, but with constantly gaining force, the great era of prosperity that lasted until the depression of 1884, followed by the panic of 1893, during which time such a large part of American industry was founded.

CHAPTER X

CLIMBING UP AGAIN

WITH the resumption of specie payments on New Year's Day, 1879, business at once began to get better. We had gone through more than five very lean years—lean not because it was necessary or inevitable that they should have been lean, but lean simply because people did not have confidence.

We had not been on a gold basis. Gold is the only reliable medium of exchange that we know. For ages past it has been the symbol of wealth, and whether or not it is the best symbol for wealth (for business is mainly done on credit based upon proved productive capacity), nevertheless, the human race will have to be considerably altered before its psychology will comprehend wealth in any form other than gold or in something that can be changed into gold. I do not pretend to say how much actual influence upon the trade of the country the restoration of the gold standard had. It would probably not be difficult to arrange the statistics, but we did not think in 1879 of the economic effect of the restoration of our currency to the approved basis of international exchange. What everyone had thought during the soft money period (excepting, of course, the fiat money enthusiasts who equally, of course, were not in business—the proponents of currency changes are rarely in business) was:

"How can I make a commitment when I do not know how I am going to be paid? I may be paid in worthless money—therefore I am not going to take a chance."

After the gold standard was restored the same man said:

"Now I know that I can get real money for whatever I do—therefore I will do something."

It was this return of confidence that brought good business. Looking back over all of the various recurrent depressions in business I find that they come about largely through the lack of confidence and they leave with the renewal of confidence. It is a trite but a true saying that business is built upon confidence.

During those lean years few men had full confidence in their fellows. It was extremely difficult to borrow money in the banks. It was extremely difficult to secure any kind of credit accommodation. Everyone wanted cash. Credit was, to a considerable extent, withdrawn. Business is largely done on credit. Credit does not exist without confidence. Therefore without confidence there is no credit—and little business.

The increase of business in this country is largely

in proportion to the increase in confidence—that is, in credit. One can see this everywhere. Years ago when the farmer was not prosperous he objected to taking a cheque: he insisted upon money. Now farmers almost everywhere will take cheques and often prefer them to money. If I go into a community where it is difficult to cash a cheque, I know at once that I am not in a prosperous, progressive community but in one where suspicion instead of confidence prevails. As suspicion rises business disappears.

Another element that prevented business on a large scale was the uncertainty concerning prices. They had reached the top in '73 and then had tumbled—although not with the swiftness of the closing months of 1920. Everyone is afraid to buy on a declining market. They will buy at the best from hand to mouth and at the worst will postpone buying altogether. But since the price ultimately depends upon the demand it must in the larger way be considered as a result and not as a cause. It is the buyer who makes the price. During the periods of large demand the seller sometimes thinks he makes the price, and he does to a degree. Eventually he makes it so high that people stop buying and then for a while the seller really does make the price. He refuses to sell below a certain figure; he insists that he is not going to lose money, and then he gathers his fellows around him and they all agree that under no circumstances are they going to lose money. And by some tomfoolery or other, be it open-price association, trade association, or what not, they solemnly restrict production and hold out for price. They make the price—but nobody buys.

They keep right on making the price until one fine morning some intelligent man awakes to the fact that business does not grow out of making prices but out of selling goods; and then the whole house of cards goes a-crashing. I have seen that happen so many times that I now regard it as one of those events in nature that inevitably happen. Our business depressions come rather far apart and only a small fund of knowledge carries over from one to another. Those who hang on to prices the longest fall the hardest. And, although they may die, they never learn!

The fear of still lowering prices was quickly overcome in 1880 by the buying that grew out of the new confidence that payment could be had for what was sold. Prices always follow confidence; confidence never follows prices. Steel started up in June, 1879. That was the time when the age of steel began and ever since steel has constituted an important barometer of business.

I had done a comparatively satisfactory business during the depression and I had always been able to get money. I have always been able to get money for the reason that I have never renewed, much less left unpaid, a note. Some time later when the banks of York were exhausted by local requirements and could not give me all of the accommodation that I required, I went to New York for money and walked without introduction into the National Park Bank. I do not believe much in introductions; I think a man ought personally to be able to tell what he is and not have to depend on another man saying it for him. I asked to see the president and the cashier; I told them what I wanted and we chatted a little while. The nature of my business forced to me sell largely on fairly long-term notes given to me by farmer customers or country distributors, and it was these notes that I wanted to discount.

The president asked me what proportion of these notes was paid at maturity. I told him that the average was about 75 per cent., that perhaps 25 per cent. renewed, but that practically all were eventually paid. My credit losses were then and always have been comparatively small. Then he asked me:

"How much do you speculate?"

I answered: "I have never speculated and never intend to speculate either in the stock market or in buying raw materials ahead of my needs, except in the latter case if I should see clearly there would be an advance in price because goods were being made at less than cost." I added that I had never made a bet in my life. "I am in business—not in gambling."

We had a little chat about speculation and he nodded: "I can see you do not drink. How much of a line do you want?"

I told him, and he gave it to me. That was my first New York banking connection and I have ever since retained it. I have never had any difficulty in being trusted anywhere, and I think this is due to the fact that, having obeyed my father's teaching never to deceive, I have always had such perfect confidence in myself that other people have shared that confidence. And I have a feeling that if ever I did deceive I should lose that confidence in myself and be unable to make people believe me. This has stood me in good stead innumerable times. Once, for instance, in making a short trip to London from Paris I found, on arriving in England, that my letter of credit from Brown, Shipley & Co. was in my trunk at the Hotel Continental in Paris. I went to the London office of Brown, Shipley & Co., told them the circumstances, and how much money I wanted. We talked awhile and they gave me the money on my simple promise to hand them my letter of credit on my return within a week.

In 1914, at the opening of the war, I was in Constantinople. All the banks had closed. They were absolutely forbidden to pay out money even on letters of credit. I hunted up the president of the Ottoman Bank and offered him a cheque on New York. He did not know me from Adam and he explained that under no circumstances could he pay out any gold, the only currency that was of any service.

"But," I said, "you owe money in New York and this is New York exchange I am giving you. Let us sit down and have a chat. Perhaps we can find a way out."

We discussed my business at home and my business abroad. I explained that I was vice-president of the Chamber of Commerce of the United States, and was on a semi-government mission, and finally he said:

"As president of this bank I cannot give you the money, but I will cash the cheque myself!"

And not only did he cash it but he gave me gold, which at that time was harder to procure in Turkey than diamonds. The cheque was not presented for payment for six or seven months afterward.

Another instance: Going to the theatre in New York with my wife and some friends I found at the box-office that I had left all my money in the safe at the hotel. I did not know that theatre ticket sellers ever trusted any one and I did not ask this one to, but as I fumbled through my pockets and found that I had no money, I asked for the tickets and merely remarked, "I will call in to-morrow at nine o'clock and pay you for them, as I left my money at the hotel." And he replied: "That is all right."

These are merely mentioned as instances among

many others I might offer that if a man never deceives he will be trusted.

Credit is a delicate and fragile thing, but I think it is open to any one who tells the truth, and any one telling the truth will not abuse credit, for he will not ask for more than he should have. If I can talk with a man for five minutes I do not want to see his credit statement. I think the intangibles are more trustworthy than the tangibles. I should not extend credit to a man I felt I could not trust no matter what kind of a statement he exhibited, and I should extend credit to a truthful man regardless of his statement, and this has worked out to my entire satisfaction.

Just before the Baring failure, in 1882 I shipped implements to the amount of $67,000 to Buenos Aires for the account of some customers whom I knew well, and who, when in this country, had been entertained at my house. Then came the big failure and I received word form the New York correspondents that I should have to wait indefinitely for payment of the account. It was a very large amount of money for me to wait for and would have given me considerable embarrassment. Therefore I went to New York, talked with the agents and asked them to communicate with my Argentine customers and see if they could not devise some method of arranging for payment. They said they did not know what they could do but they would try. In a very little while the answer came: "Pay Mr. Farquhar the full amount in cash, as we are indebted to him for personal courtesy." This is another instance of the value of making friends of your customers.

During this period of prosperity I expanded my plant to a considerable degree although I was careful not to tax my resources or to engage in any building programme which might, if the prosperity ceased, leave me short of funds. I have never believed in locking up more money than was necessary either in plant or in inventory. Both of them are but tools for doing business—they are not business—and normally I should rather have my facilities a little less than adequate for the volume of business than a little more than adequate. By 1880 about one half of our present plant was up, and during this period I moved out of the residence put up in 1863, which was right in the centre of the plant, and converted it into an office. My old bedroom is now my private office. I built that house—I was the architect and the contractor, and my workmen put it up. It is a brick house and it is still covered by the same tin roof that I put on it at the time of building. It is a particularly fine grade of what was known as "Double Cross" tin that I bought in Wales. At that time tinplate was not made in this country to any extent and iron was its base instead of steel. None of the floors in the house have had to be renewed; it has not settled; and neither has it been necessary even to repair the stone steps or the front door. I made the doors in my factory out of walnut and I believe they were the first walnut doors that had ever been used in York.

Politically the country was in rather an upset condition owing to the prevalence of unsound theories of economics, particularly touching the currency and the tariff. The Republican Party had come solidly into power and it was beginning to be realized by astute but narrow-minded politicians and manufacturers that artificial monopolies could very easily be created by means of a protective tariff. I think that this had not occurred to any one until the higher tariffs made necessary for war revenues and for paying off the war debts gave an idea of what might be done with a really high protective tariff—that under the guise of protecting infant industries some fat adult pocketbook might be created. As a student of economics and also as a business man I have never liked the idea of extreme protection and have always thoroughly agreed with Henry Clay, when he said, in advocating a tariff of only ten years' duration, that he believed that any industry which could not find itself within ten years was not worth protecting. I have always held that it is to the benefit of the people of all countries to have cheap goods and plenty of them, and that any restraint upon the ebb and flow of trade, while it may seem to help a few, really hurts the many. I have always found it perfectly

possible to sell at a profit anywhere in the world
and I do not want a tariff which is so high as to en-
courage a price-fixing combination of producers
and permit me to sell at a high price in the United
States, where competition below a certain level is
removed, and at a low price in China where I have
to meet outside competition. I think the United
States, as well as foreign countries, should have
the benefit of low prices on American goods.

I bring this up at this moment because I have
noticed that after each business depression there
appears one strong movement for a high tariff and
another strong movement for what is called "cheap
money." A period of so-called prosperity usually
results in a greater or less amount of inflation and
promotes the notion that credit, which is a means
of interchanging things, can somehow be made
to substitute for capital—which is a means of
making things. The human political and business
mind seems to travel through cycles and after
every business depression comes the incessant, un-
reasoned, unreasoning, blatant demand for a high
tariff and cheap money. We have never yet as a
people failed to respond to the politician who promises something for nothing. But of this, more
later.

Both Garfield and Blaine were exceptionally
brilliant men, and I have always felt that if Garfield
had not been assassinated within four months after
his inauguration as President in 1881, he would

have saved the country from some of the economic fallacies which it was fast embracing. Of Blaine I saw a good deal later.

We were passing out of the period of individual ownership and into the period of corporate organization, and among the interesting individualists I would mention Johns Hopkins of Baltimore, a distant cousin by marriage, and one of the most peculiar figures of all time.

Johns Hopkins had two special interests. The first was money, and the second his plans for a hospital and university to which he purposed to bequeath his fortune. He seldom displayed human traits but he had a most uncanny faculty for telling in advance whether or not a man would pay his bills and an equally uncanny faculty for economical living. He told me that the secret of success was:

"Do not waste anything. Make everything you do, and every cent you have, count. The reason why people are poor or unsuccessful is that they waste. Any one can succeed who does not waste."

And he did not waste anything. He started as a clerk in a store and saved about nine tenths of his wages. When only a boy he began lending out his money at interest and at high interest too, for in those days 10 per cent. or more was not an unusual interest rate to pay. He had practically no expenses and before he reached middle life was a rich man and became president of the Merchants' Bank, of Baltimore. Then he began a practice that was known in London but nearly unknown in this country—that of endorsing notes for a fee.

I never heard of any one who loved Johns Hopkins, but also I never heard of any one who ever had the shadow of a doubt of his financial integrity. He was known to be worth millions but how many millions no one knew. What everyone knew was that anything he put his name to was as good as gold. Therefore, in a very short time, in addition to lending his own money, he endorsed the paper of others for a fee ranging up to 5 per cent., and with that endorsement the paper could be discounted anywhere. "Johns Hopkins' Paper" was a staple investment and I recall that our banks in York used to buy it freely. He was interested in the Baltimore & Ohio Railroad and made a great deal of money out of it, and as an instance of his remarkable credit standing he personally endorsed one loan of several million dollars by the railroad, and on his endorsement the securities were sold in France. I do not recall any other case where the securities of a railway corporation were sold upon the strength of a personal endorsement. As far as his name on paper was concerned he was not an individual but an institution.

As I have said, his credit judgment was uncanny. He would endorse the paper of a man whom everyone else had turned down, and the notes would be paid at maturity. He would refuse to endorse notes of a man whom most people considered a good risk, and that man would fail. I asked him how he formed his judgment, for, like most men of that time, he had few records, no assistants, and kept the data in his head. He answered:

"I never endorse the paper of any one whom I do not know. I watch the habits of every man in business hereabouts. I find out how they do business. If they waste, I do not bother with them further. I can see by the way they act whether or not they are going to make good. If I feel that they are going to make good I will endorse the paper up to the amount I think they are good for. I do not want any report of any kind. I depend on my own judgment and that judgment does not fail me."

He was a hard, austere sort of a man and I think not unlike, in habits and personality, Stephen Girard, who also was unloved and unregarded excepting for his money, and yet he put all of the money he made into that remarkable institution Girard College. Johns Hopkins fully formulated the plan of the university that he wanted to found. He got his pleasure in life out of money-making and planning the hospital and the university to which his money was to go. He was influenced in this, I think, by George Peabody, who built the Peabody Institute in Baltimore—an example of how this good deed of one man encourages another.

He seldom went anywhere or did anything to

attract notice. He was a strong, rugged character and not easily fooled. He regarded the people who came to him for money more as credit risks than as human beings and those who came to him for other purposes than money he had little regard for. I knew him and we had interesting chats. He might have loaned me money if I had asked him for it, but I never did and never would. It has been one of my principles never to borrow money excepting from banks in a business way, and although Johns Hopkins was more of an institution for lending money than he was a relative and I am entirely certain would not have cared in the least for the relationship had I applied for money, yet I fortunately never found any occasion so urgent that I cared to ask him. I once asked him for advice, however, and he told me I would find Philip and Samuel Small of York my best advisers.

He had a single room as an office with a plain wooden table and a few hard, plain chairs. I think that $15 or $20 would have been a large estimate on the value of his office furnishing. I said to him one day:

"Cousin Johns, you spend most of your time in this office, why don't you buy yourself at least a reasonable amount of comfort?"

"No, no," he answered, "it would be waste to have anything in here that I can get along without, and anyway it is better to live simply and to play poor. In an office like this people come in and ask for subscriptions. They see me and they see my office and they are satisfied if I give them fifty cents. If I had a better furnished office they might want as much as five dollars."

One of the town worthies that he held up to me as the maker of a considerable fortune by mere economy was Moses Shepherd.

"There is an example," he used to say, "of what a man can do who does not waste. He has only a little grocery store, he lives in it, he does not have the expense of a family, and he never eats anything more expensive than crackers and cheese, and yet he is worth several hundred thousand dollars. He has all that money because he saves all that he makes."

Shepherd was another curious character who loved money for itself. He never had anything but a small store. I understand that he speculated to some extent but certainly he never spent any money and when he died he left a large fortune to the founding of the Shepherd Asylum. Russell Sage had something of these same characteristics. He also loved money for itself alone and piled it up feeling a kind of sardonic glee as to what was going to be done with it after he died. I have known quite a number of men who found their recreation, so to speak, in investing money. Judge Spottswood, of the Supreme Court of Pennsylvania, was one of these. I asked him:

"What do you do to amuse yourself outside of your judicial duties?"

"My principal interest is in investments," he answered. "I buy things that pay their dividends quarterly, reinvest the money, and," he said, smacking his lips, "Great God, but it rolls up!"

A very different kind of man was Ross Winans, who was another of the great citizens of Baltimore. He and my Uncle, John Elgar, turned out the first of the coal-burning locomotives. When they built their first locomotive Winans insisted that the wheels would not have sufficient tractive power to haul a train up grade and that it would be necessary to put cogs in the centre of the track as they do now in vermicular railways. My uncle, who was an inventor and a scientist, knew that the friction increased with the pressure but Winans insisted on the cog wheel and it was put on. But before the first trial, my uncle drove the key out of the cog wheel on the axle so that it would run loose and after the trial, when Winans was congratulating him on the result and felicitating himself on his foresight in providing the cog, he was astonished to find that as far as tractive force had been concerned the cog was an ornament.

Winans had started as a mechanic and eventually became a locomotive builder with the rise of the Baltimore & Ohio Railroad. His machine shop at Baltimore was the first that I had ever seen and probably led me into becoming a machinist. He was an immense, kindly, patriarchal sort of a man, and the first time I called at the factory as a boy he took me through personally and invited me to his house for dinner with my uncle John Elgar. That factory had the first iron roof I had ever seen, but it had wooden rafters and I asked him why he supported a fireproof roof with such a highly inflammable substance as wood. He answered:

"You cannot set fire to a single stick of timber. You must have at least two sticks together before you can have a fire. Therefore these beams widely separated are just as fireproof as iron and they are a great deal lighter and cheaper."

It had never occurred to me before that a single stick of wood will not burn.

Ross Winans' son, Thomas Winans, continued the business and made a large fortune building the railway for the Russian Government from Moscow to St. Petersburg. He told me that, after they had carefully worked out the plans for the road, Czar Nicholas looked at the map they had drawn, and then, taking a ruler, drew a straight line from Moscow to St. Petersburg and told them that that was the line the railroad should take. And that was the line the railroad did take, of course, at an enormous increase in expense. They so faithfully followed the Czar's line that they had to build many of the bridges diagonally across rivers!

Thomas Winans took pleasure in life and built himself a great house on Lombard Street, Baltimore, with enormous gardens that were the wonder of the town. On his return from abroad he brought with him a number of nude statues that he put around the house grounds. The Baltimore papers attacked the morality of the display of these naked statues and Thomas became so incensed that he built a great high brick wall around the entire estate in the heart of the city, and thereafter spent much of his time at his country home, and the citizens were very much distressed at being deprived of the enjoyment of these beautiful works of art which had been visible through the iron fence before the wall was erected.

CHAPTER XI

I KNEW President Johnson slightly, and, I am sorry to say, had a very poor opinion of him. Also I knew James G. Blaine, Charles Sumner, and most of the leading figures at the close of the war, but my closest friend among men of note was Judge Jeremiah S. Black, Attorney General and later Secretary of State in President Buchanan's Cabinet. I had known Judge Black casually before and during the war, but when he came to York to live in the early seventies I learned to know him intimately. Many amusing ancedotes were told of him. Once in returning from a trip of about a week, Mrs. Black, in looking over his wardrobe said:

"Where are the shirts I gave you?"

He answered:

"Why you told me to put another one on every morning, which I did."

She found him clothed with the six shirts. He was one of the most interesting characters of the period—a man of parts, of a lovable nature, albeit blunt and outspoken in his opinions. It is related of him that on one occasion, when he was conducting a case before Judge Chambers in the Franklin County Court, he became very severe, and even abusive. Judge Chambers said:

"Black, you will have to apologize for your language."

Black replied, quoting from Othello, "Haply I am Black, your Honour, and have not the soft parts of speech that chamberers have."

This set the Judge to laughing and the point was not pressed. Black was a Shakespearean scholar, quick witted and full of apt quotations. He had the happy faculty of saying things which although sharp did not rankle. People could take things from him which from another would make them furiously angry. Once he gave the United States Supreme Court a lecture for lack of knowledge of the law. In describing a proposed bond issue he said: "Not satisfied with mulcting the present generation, they reach their long felon fingers down into the pockets of posterity." Another of his sentences comes to mind: "Justice moves with a leaden heel, but you will find it will strike with an iron hand."

Judge Black came to York from Somerset County. Much of his practice was in Philadelphia, Harrisburg, and Washington, and he took a fancy to York as a midway point from which he could conveniently reach any of them. He built the first modern country residence near York. He purchased the estate in 1861 just before the Civil

War. No one expected payment in those days
till the 1st of April, and he promised to pay the
owner on that date in 1862. In the meantime
the war had broken out, specie payments had
ceased, and the greenback had been made the
legal tender. But he bought gold, paying the
debt in that metal, saying gold was the currency
at the time he bought the land, and he would not
feel as if it belonged to him if he paid in anything
else but gold. Although a loyal Democrat, had
he lived he would not have followed Mr. Bryan in
that gentleman's free-silver vagaries. People did
not believe it possible that anybody not engaged
in agriculture could really prefer to live in the
country. His house occupied a beautiful spot
on a ridge of hills to the south overlooking the
town of York, and was named "Brockie," that
being the name of the previous owner of the land.
The original house burned down some years ago
and was replaced by a beautiful residence be-
longing to Mr. Elmer Smith, one of our leading
manufacturers, who had purchased the property
from the Black estate.

My first real acquaintance with the Judge came
about in this way. He drove up in front of my
office one day, got out, came in, and asked me to
drive out in the country with him to see a spring
and tell him if there was water enough to supply
a house by using a ram—that he thought of buying the place on the hill, and the only question

was whether there would be enough water to fill the reservoir which he proposed to erect to supply the house. He said that he had been told that I was the proper person to see.

I said all we wanted was a watch and a quart measure. I told the Judge that I knew him from his likeness in the papers, which I had seen many a time. I got in the buggy with him, and he remarked:

"If you want to stop and get your coat you can, but it is so warm you would be more comfortable without it."

"Judge," I said, "I am not ashamed to be seen riding with you; you have the reputation of being an honest lawyer, and I suppose an honest lawyer is just as good as any other honest man."

This amused him, and he put his arm around me and said:

"I guess we shall be good friends."

We went to the spring and I measured the flow. I told him it would take about nine quarts to give one quart by a ram. We found that there was plenty of water. When we got through and had talked over where he should place his home, we lay down under a tree and discussed literature and told stories until about 11 o'clock at night. When we came back he said:

"Look here, if I build a house out there I want you for a neighbour. You ought to live in the country.   Will you build a house on one of those neighbouring hills?"

I replied: "Well, there is just one objection to it, Judge. I haven't the money to spare. My business needs all my funds, and I don't feel able to build another home."

"I recently received a large fee for conducting a case," he replied—the largest fee, it was said, that had been paid any lawyer in the country up to that time—"you see money comes easy to me, and I will lend you the money or give it to you. I want you for a neighbour."

Of course, I would not accept a gift, but eventually I did build a house on the hill, and we became the closest of friends—we always spent our Sunday evenings together when at home. He was one of the great jurists of the country, had been Chief Justice of the Supreme Court of Pennsylvania before entering Buchanan's Cabinet, and his country home was visited by several notables of the day, including Garfield. Judge Black died in my arms, and his death was one of the greatest blows I ever received. He was a great reader, a fine speaker and writer, and one of the most interesting conversationalists I ever knew. He died with a prayer on his lips that his faithful wife should be preserved and comforted. I telegraphed the news of his death to the national Attorney General and the Secretary of State, then Messrs. Brewster and Freylinghuysen, and they ordered all of the office buildings of their two departments to be draped in mourning. To Judge Black's house came a number of the noted men of the time and there I met many of them, among them James A. Garfield and James G. Blaine.

Blaine had a marvellous faculty for remembering people. His friends claimed that he never forgot any one whom he had once met and spoken to. I had heard of this and once, before I had ever been introduced to him, I determined to test 'it. I met him coming out of his house at Bar Harbor and said:

"Don't you remember meeting me at Altoona where you made an address?"

He shook his head as he replied: "No, if I had met you I should remember it."

Then I went on to quote from his address and he answered:

"Yes, your quotation is exact but I have never met you before." He was absolutely positive and absolutely correct.

One of the ties that united Judge Black and myself was a common love of poetry and good literature. Being blest with a good memory, I have no difficulty in repeating long poems to-day. Frequently the words of some poem which I have not thought of since my youth will come to mind and I can repeat pages of it without a break, so tenaciously has it been stored away in my memory. It has been of real help to remember some heroic

lines at times when there was plenty to discourage.
The love of reading is a good stabilizer of character,
and the learning of poetry by heart an excellent
training of the memory.   It seems to me in these
modern days that the problem of reading has become more and more that of selection.   There is no
dearth of good books to be readily obtained by any
one who wishes to read.   I often wish the time were
twice as long so that I could read more of the good
things that come to my desk, and yet I must now
depend upon someone to read to me, since my eyes
will not admit of any extended use.   Books have
become to me, in that intimate and personal way
which is so enticing to the true book-lover, "the
ghosts of my former friends."   I must take them
for the most part through the voice of another,
and lose thereby much of their fine flavour.

Astronomy has always had a fascination for me.
Many hours of my youth were spent in gazing at
the stars, locating the constellations, reading about
the heavens.   And then I always kept in mind the
necessity of self-training.   So few people think
of that.   You must keep your own company as
long as you live, and how important it is to have
that company congenial, someone you can respect,
so that if you have no other company you will
have the inner resources within yourself to make
the time profitable.   A man must be decent if he
is to sense the full flavour of human relations.
For instance, a libertine has no real pleasure in

the society of young girls. His mind is sensual, spoiled, corrupted—he cannot understand or appreciate the delicate beauty and fineness of innocence.

I knew Henry Ward Beecher slightly—and of course by reputation. I never passed a Sunday in New York without going to hear him, although I often had to stand, for it was a common thing for all the seats to be taken. One was sorry when Beecher stopped. He was a wonderfully attractive speaker and a most interesting personality. Most of the sermons of that day were about hell. Beecher eliminated hell from his sermons; came out flat-footed against the conception of a hell, and said there could not be both hell and God, and he preferred to believe in God. I was indignant at the charges of immoral conduct against Beecher; I knew they must be false. No one who really knew and loved Beecher could for a moment doubt his integrity and purity.

Moncure Conway was a noted preacher and author. He was another of my warm friends. Just about seventy years ago my father in returning one evening took from his pocket a memorandum book that he said he had picked up in the road. He read some interesting items, from which he gathered that the writer was a young Methodist preacher temporarily located in the neighbourhood. We wished to meet him personally and so sent word that he could have the book by calling for it at our home. He called and spent the evening—and many other evenings afterward. He was already a graduate of Dickinson College in Carlisle, Pennsylvania. The library which Andrew Carnegie gave to this college some years ago was named Conway Hall, in honour of him. My father became deeply interested in Conway, and suggested his taking a course at Harvard College, where he would meet many congenial spirits. This he did, and the friendship with my father was continued. My father visited him at the College several times, and it was during these trips that he made the acquaintance of Emerson, Longfellow, Thoreau, the Alcotts, and others known as the Concord School of Philosophers. Moncure Conway remained a friend of our family and of me until his death. At one time he had a chapel in London which was attended by John Bright and many other notables. My father visited him there, as I did also on two occasions. On Conway's return to New York we always visited him at his home on Fifty-Ninth Street. I recollect that one Sunday evening his daughter Mildred told me she was going down to her East Side Sunday School and invited me to accompany her. I found a very interesting audience, composed of people of all nationalities: Jews, Christians, Catholics, and Protestants. She was much interested in trying to improve their condition, giving them lessons in dressmaking, cooking, etc. As we walked home I asked where the money came from to sustain the institution, as it must have cost considerable to keep it going and I knew her father could not spare the money. She told me it was given by a friend of her father's who did not wish his name divulged, but she finally told me his name with the understanding that it should not be mentioned. The generous donor has passed away, and there is no objection now to giving his name—Jacob Schiff, the great New York banker. It was simply one of that splendid man's many benefactions.

I attended Mr. Conway's funeral services at the house of his son Eustace in New York, sitting with Mr. and Mrs. Carnegie, who were his warm friends. Conway's autobiography is deeply interesting and widely read.

My introduction to Professor Henry, the Director of the Smithsonian Institution in Washington, came about through my uncle, Benjamin Hallowell, at a meeting in which they discussed the progress of the world and the great inventions of the past, present, and probable future. They decided that we could not expect as much in the next half century as in the last. Since then we have had the telephone, electric railways, automobile, typewriter, aeroplane, wireless telegraphy, submarines, internal combustion engines, and countless things which have astonished the world! What will the coming half century bring forth?

I was once with Graham Bell at a dinner, and while there we fell to discussing whether the telephone could ever be used commercially—this was about 1877. The majority of those present said No, it would be only a toy to amuse people. Theodore Vail, one of the guests, said it could be used, that there was a great future in it, and he would undertake to form its future. They afterward made an arrangement by which Vail should take hold of the telephone. Vail, of course, sold stock, and it was very lucky for him that he could not sell as much stock as he wanted to, for what he kept for himself eventually became very valuable. I remember that George Small, of York, brother and partner of Latimer Small, and then in charge of the branch of the Small business in Baltimore, told the story of an acquaintance of his who was dissipated and had run through his fortune until he had but about a thousand dollars left. He told Mr. Small that he was going to spend his last thousand in one great jag and then give up. Mr. Small advised him to take a flyer in the stock market and buy this new telephone stock. The young fellow asked what that was, and on having it explained said:

"That is so absurd it appeals to my fancy, and I will buy a thousand dollars' worth of stock."

He did so, and it made him a fortune. When I last heard of him he was a rich man.

The first time I talked through the telephone

was at the Centennial Exposition in Philadelphia. My brother-in-law was with me, and he took the transmitter at one end of the line in another building and I took the receiver. It seemed to me one of the most astonishing things man could conceive of, but no one then seemed to imagine it would become one of the world's greatest time savers.

I have known the presidents more or less well since Cleveland, whom I knew quite well and have already tried to portray. I knew and admired General Grant. I have already spoken of him. Following Grant was Hayes. I frequently visited President Hayes. President Hayes's title to the presidency was affirmed by the Supreme Court, but it was well known that he did not really receive the majority of the votes cast, as he was counted out in South Carolina, Florida, and Louisiana. Of course, the Supreme Court decision settled the matter, although it took some time for the opposition to become reconciled to this, and Hayes's sensibilities suffered from the fact that the election was of doubtful validity. President Hayes was a graduate of Kenyon College, Gambier, Ohio, which college, by the way, gave me my LL.D. degree. He was a man of high character and charming personality.

I have already referred to President Garfield, whom I first met at the home of Judge Black. He was one of the most attractive characters I ever knew, an eloquent speaker and well read.

I became attached to President Garfield and his family; I attended Garfield's funeral, travelling in the funeral train, and later attended the marriage of two of his children at Mentor, Ohio. I was deeply impressed by Secretary Blaine's funeral oration, delivered in the House of Representatives, the latter part of which I have never forgotten. It goes thus:

As the end drew near his early craving for the sea returned. The stately mansion of power had been to him but a wearisome hospital of pain; he begged to be taken from its prison walls, its oppressive, stifling air, its homelessness and hopelessness. Gently, quietly, the love of a great people bore the pale sufferer to the longed for healing of the sea, there to live or to die as God should will, within sight of its heaving billows, within sound of its manifold voices. With wan, fevered face, tenderly lifted to the cooling breeze he looked out wistfully upon the ocean's changing wonders, upon the far off sail whitening in the morning light, upon the restless waves rolling shoreward to break and die beneath the noonday sun, upon the red clouds of evening arching low to the horizon, and the serene and shining pathway of the stars. Let us believe that his dying eyes read a mystic meaning which only the rapt and parting soul may know. Let us hope that in the silence of a receding world he heard the great waves breaking on a farther shore and felt already upon his wasted brow the breath of the eternal morning.

Blaine loved him. Garfield was a very lovely character, very interesting, and the whole world was stirred by his death. The fishing smacks in England put their flags at half mast. He was very human, very attractive and sweet in his disposition. The assassination of Garfield seemed to touch the whole world—his hard fight for life and his death by the sea which he loved. He was removed from the White House in the easiest riding Pullman coach that could be found, with pressed paper wheels, and the crowds which lined the route all the way were as silent as death. When they arrived at the seashore, people had come down from New York; crowds were standing silently as the train slowly passed by. An Englishman who owned a cottage at Elberon gave it up to the use of the President, and they laid a railroad right over the lawns and through the front yards so that the car which bore him could be taken to the door. All was in charge of his faithful secretary, J. Stanley Brown, who afterward married Garfield's daughter Mollie. I went to see the President while he was sick. Mollie, his daughter, was then about eleven years old; the others were boys —James and Harry.

After Garfield's death I became quite well acquainted with President Arthur. He was very polite and attractive. In calling on him once at the White House his secretary said he had just gone in to dress for dinner. I asked him to take my card in and was invited to come in and sit in his room while he dressed—which shows how unconventional he was. We had a good talk.

I never could get very close to President Harrison. I don't think any one did. But he impressed me as a very able man of a judicial temperament, one on whom we could rely, and probably under his reserve a very likeable fellow. His speeches throughout the country were always admirable, and his administration on the whole was successful, but the country became disgusted with the inordinate tariff rates, and that was the main issue raised in the second election of Cleveland.

Of Cleveland—my warm friend—I have already spoken. He was followed by McKinley, who had a charming personality. I grew to be very fond of him. I have already written an account of the reappointment of W. I. Buchanan as Minister to the Argentine. I called on the U. S. Senator from Iowa to get his approval of the reappointment of Buchanan, in order to assist Mr. McKinley in getting release from a promise made for the appointment of another man, for which the President seemed very grateful. The news of his assassination in Buffalo was a great shock. An account of it was telegraphed me by his secretary, Mr. Cortelyou, in the evening, followed by a message every morning and evening until his death. I attended his funeral, entering the church with the Hon. Myron Herrick, our present Ambassador to France. It was most impressive.

Then we had President Roosevelt—always a personal friend. I never went to Washington without visiting him. He was unquestionably one of the best informed and most attractive men I ever knew. As an instance, there was a meeting of ornithologists at the New Willard Hotel. One of them made a criticism of something President Roosevelt had said about a certain bird. I asked him if he was acquainted with the President. He said he had not that honour but added that he would like to meet him. I wrote on the back of one of my cards an introduction to the President, with the remark that the bearer did not agree with him about this bird. The card gained him the desired audience at once, and he told me in the evening that he had had a very pleasant chat with the President, who knew far more about that bird than he did—and, as for that matter, about everything else.

On another occasion I was kept waiting awhile, very properly, by the doorkeeper because the President had a Senator with him. The President came to the door with the Senator and asked me how long I had been waiting. I told him about half an hour, and he said:

"Why did you not come in as I told you?"

I answered that the doorkeeper would not admit me. He laughed, and asked:

"Why didn't you knock him down?"

Once Senator Root came in with a new ambassador while I was talking to the President.

He motioned me to take a seat, which I did.   They conversed for an hour and a half by the clock— one of the most interesting hours I ever spent in my life.   As they went out the President said to himself:

"Well, I am now through for the day."   Turning round, he noticed me and said: "Why, what are you doing here?"

I told him: "I took a seat as you directed."

He said: "You have heard some important state secrets."

"Oh, yes," I answered, "but they will remain secrets with me."   He threw his arm round my shoulders and said, "I know that."   We had a delightful talk.

Just before the nomination of Taft I saw the President and I said:

"It is a pity that you promised not again to be a candidate—there would have been no trouble about your renomination and you could have finished up the work you are engaged in."

He seemed to agree with me, but said he would recommend Taft as his successor, and wanted me to support him, which I promised to do, but I told him I did not know Mr. Taft.   He said: "Go over and see the Secretary."   I went to the War Department.   The Secretary was busy, but when he heard that I had been sent by the President, he invited me in at once and we were friends from that hour.   I did not think Mr. Roosevelt treated

President Taft entirely fairly when Taft ran for the second nomination, and told him so. He replied: "The people seemed to want me to be a candidate; twelve governors have called on me insisting it was my duty, and I feel it is my duty to do what the people of the country want."

I insisted that it would hurt his reputation, that another election could not add to it, and then we had our first breach or misunderstanding. After the nomination of Taft and his defeat, I met the Colonel's son, Theodore, Jr., at Bertron, Griscom & Co's bank, where he was engaged at the time, and he asked me why I did not drop in to see his father at the *Outlook* office as I used to do, adding that his father had spoken of it the day before. I said:

"Oh, I doubt if he wants to see me."

Theodore went to the telephone booth, called up his father, told him that I was there, and I distinctly heard the familiar word, "Delighted," in his father's voice, as I was standing at the door. He turned around and said:

"Father will be delighted to see you."

I was never met more cordially in my life than when I called on the Colonel at the *Outlook* office *en route* up town, and our friendship lasted till the great man's death.

Of course, I am fond of Mr. Taft—everyone is who knows him—and I often saw him. He spoke of me as an adviser of presidents in one of his speeches, and seemed glad to talk with me on various subjects. His dream always was to enter the Supreme Court. Mr. McKinley had promised him the appointment when there was a vacancy, but told him that he could save ten thousand men by going to the Philippines and settling matters there. This was shortly after the acquisition of the islands. Mr. Taft deemed it his duty to go, and made a great success. The natives liked him. All over the island they tacked boards to trees on which they wrote: "We love Taft." He was also successful in making arrangements as to the Church property with the Pope; he was always successful wherever harmony was needed. The wish of his life is now fulfilled as Chief Justice of the Supreme Court. In speaking of the appointment to President Harding, I was glad to find he agreed with me and had already made up his mind about it.

Of course when the Great War broke out I felt it my duty to do what I could in the common cause; I spent considerable time in Washington, where I saw much of Secretaries McAdoo, Lane, Baker, and Daniels, who were all my friends. Secretary McAdoo told me that he would have liked to have me as a member of the Shipping Board, but we compromised by my promising to act in an advisory capacity. I was received very cordially by the Board when I visited Washington. I reminded them that the Government had never manufactured ships, only built them one at a time, and that we wanted a man of vision to take hold of emergency ship building. I was asked whom I would recommend. I said: "Charlie Schwab, General Goethals, and Henry Ford are all men of vision." They asked me to talk with them over the long-distance telephone. Mr. Schwab said he was overwhelmed with shipping business for the Government at his works in Bethlehem and it would not be to the advantage of the Government for him to leave. General Goethals said: "I am a soldier and am ready to obey orders."

Henry Ford was not at home, but wrote me afterward an appreciative letter.

General Goethals was appointed, and there developed a good deal of friction ending in the retirement of the Chairman of the Board and of the General. I begged the General to stick, but he thought it best to resign. I then did my best to induce Mr. Schwab to take the place and with the help of the President finally succeeded. Mr. Schwab told me that General Goethals's plans were all good and that he would work on the same line. I had the pleasure of telling this to the General— which seemed greatly to please him.

I of course saw as much of President Wilson as he had time for. He was a very busy man. His addresses and letters were classics, and his conception of the League of Nations to put an end to war was great and could have been carried through with a few reservations had there not been so much personal antagonism.

My friendship with President Taft continued after his retirement. I recollect walking down Chestnut Street with him from the Bellevue-Stratford Hotel to Independence Hall when the League to Enforce Peace was started, a movement in which I took a very great interest. Mr. Taft was deeply interested in the Versailles League, made some good suggestions which were adopted, and sincerely regretted that our country failed to join; since more than two thirds of Congress favoured a league of nations the President and the Foreign Relations Committee ought to have compromised their differences.

And now we have Warren G. Harding, whose administration promises well. He is admirably equipped by a knowledge of business and political experience in the Congress of the United States. A knowledge of politics is essential to the best work of a chief executive. I have met Mr. Harding personally a number of times. He manifested not only willingness but eagerness to hear what I had to say. He has gathered around him an exceptionally strong cabinet, and I prophesy a successful administration. The great work for which he will probably stand highest is the epoch-making Limitation of Armaments Conference which is at this writing reaching a successful close.

A prominent member of the previous administration told me that with such strong men around him, Harding could not fail to have a good administration, especially mentioning his admiration for Hughes and Hoover. Mr. Hoover I look upon as one of the greatest men living in the world to-day. Judged by Lincoln's criterion that the greatest man is the best man and the best man is the one who has done the most good, Hoover certainly overtops most men. Mr. Hoover has Lincoln's idea that we are in the world to do good, and that we should make it the main object of our lives to do the most good we can.

Two of my family were in government service. Edward Farquhar was assistant librarian in the Patent Office, a position he attained at the age of twenty-two and held until his death. He was quite a noted scholar and scientist in Washington and understood thirteen languages. We were constant correspondents, and I feel his loss deeply to the present day.

Another brother, Henry Farquhar, was in the Coast Survey, statistician of the Agricultural Department, and in the Census Bureau until his late retirement on reaching 70 this year. My sister Ellen, at 85 years of age, is still in good health at the old home, enjoying her flowers, books, and many friends. My brother Allan, the youngest, remained on the farm, but is secretary of the

Mutual Fire Insurance Company of Montgomery County, which has a large clientele.

Of my sons, William E. Farquhar is a contractor in New York, and doing well. My son Percival has an international reputation as a promoter of large enterprises. Among other things he was president of the Brazil Railway Co. and of the Mamore Railway Co. in Brazil, and the railroad from Santa Barros to Guatemala City, called the Guatemala R. R., and was active in building the Cuba R. R. from Havana to Santiago, running nearly the length of the island.

I have always been deeply interested in the subject of the peace of the world. I regard war as the greatest enemy to business as well as to moral and intellectual advancement. I attended the Hague Conference in 1907, where I was entertained by Mr. W. I. Buchanan, ex-Secretary Foster, and others. I was at the laying of the cornerstone of the Carnegie Palace of Peace at The Hague. I attended an arbitration conference in London some years before the outbreak of the war, where I met Lloyd George, and had the honour of being on the same platform with him. I also was introduced to Mr. Asquith and had the pleasure of dining with him twice. I met a number of prominent Englishmen and was entertained by Lord Brassey and the Duke of Northumberland.

In my visit to London in 1884 I had letters of introduction to Justin M'Carthy and was invited to his home. He was one of the very interesting men. I also met his son Justin H. M'Carthy. One of the most interesting events of that trip was a meeting with Mr. Gladstone. He was to speak in a hall of the Waverley Market House in Edinburgh. Tickets had been sold to the full capacity of the great hall. They told me it was impossible to get a seat. I called at the home of the chairman of the committee of arrangements and told him I had come on purpose to hear Mr. Gladstone. He smiled, handed me a ticket, and said: "This will admit you all right."

I joined the crowd. The police told me the hall was already jammed full and they could not admit any one, that there were evidently more tickets sold than there were seats. I told an officer I had been given a ticket by the Chairman of the Committee on Arrangements. He asked to see it, and when I handed it to him he called an officer, who took me by the arm and escorted me around to the door leading to the platform, where I was given a seat right by Mr. Gladstone, Lord Rosebery, Lord Rhea, and several others to whom I was introduced. I had a very interesting chat with Mr. Gladstone before the meeting commenced. Among other things I asked him what was the happiest time of life. He said:

"You must ask an older man than I am—interests increase with gathering years."

I have felt this to be true in my own case.

At the hotel I met a man that evening who spoke to me and said he had seen me on the platform, that he himself was at the extreme end of the hall, but could hear every word Mr. Gladstone said just as well as though he had been right by. Gladstone had a wonderful voice which would carry all over the largest building.

I was very much attracted to Lloyd George. His head, next to that of Daniel Webster, is about the strongest, most leonine that I ever saw. I met him again at the Hotel Crillon in Paris in 1916 when I went with the Industrial Commission to France, during which time we visited the trenches and were in Rheims while that city was under bombardment. This was the year before our country declared war. Lloyd George said:

"The last time I saw you we were talking for peace, I remember; now we are fighting for it. What are you doing?"

I told him we were investigating, but that there was no question but that we would be assisting them very soon, that the indications all pointed to it. Lloyd George I regard as a wonderful character, probably the ablest statesman now living in the world.

The numerous societies to which I have belonged have brought me into contact with a great many interesting men known in literature and science. Although still closely identified with the business here, my interests extend largely to outside matters, especially the Chamber of Commerce of the United States, one of the most important influences for good in the country, wholly non-political, interested in better legislation, better transportation, housing, civics, and everything else that contributes to the welfare of the country.

For many years I had felt the need of such an organization, as had many other business men. I took it up with the Secretary of Commerce, Hon. Oscar Straus, and later on with Secretary Nagel and President Taft. I found strong sympathy for the movement. Its organization commenced with a large gathering from all parts of the country in Washington called by Secretary of Commerce Nagel, during Taft's administration, where Harry A. Wheeler, of Chicago was elected first president. I was made vice president for the East. At the first meeting of the directors, Mr. Wheeler being late, I took the Chair. We had no money, nothing even to pay for the stationery used, and it was proposed that the directors should each pledge a thousand dollars. Our forty directors, who are prominent men from all parts of the country, serve without pay. I have attended every directors' meeting since organization—when I have been in the country. I have never heard one word spoken with any motive other than the public welfare, nor politics ever discussed. We get through a great deal of business in a very short time. I have often thought that Congress could take lessons from us.

CHAPTER XII

THE REASONS FOR BUSINESS

IN 1884 the country was again in the midst of a business depression. We had spurted mightily in business for five years, prices had gone up, and as always on a rapidly rising market, men began to speculate by buying ahead of their needs. During those five years it was all but impossible to talk to a business man without having him tell you that he had, by wise buying, a profit of so many thousand dollars on his inventory. There were no poor buyers.

In a rising market only a genius can be a poor buyer, for by the time he has the goods delivered prices have risen so that he can show a profit on inventory. Why any one should want to brag about a profit on inventory, I cannot imagine. The purpose of manufacturing or merchandising is to buy and sell with whatever service may be required to make the selling price higher than the buying price. It has always been my practice to be conservative in purchasing beyond my needs. Only when careful study of world conditions convinced me that a rise was sure did I purchase excess stock. Ordinarily I would rather run the risk of paying the higher price than tie up my money in raw material speculation with the inevitable prospect of serious embarrassment when my valuable inventory suddenly became less valuable.

Iron and steel were steadily advancing and when I refused to commit myself on a long contract with Jones & Laughlin on the ground that the price was too high, I received a long letter from Mr. Jones, head of the firm, telling me that I was mistaken and that iron and steel would not come down, that they would probably continue to advance, and no man knew the high limit of price. On the contrary, I was sure that all signs pointed to the fact that iron and steel were too high and that prices would soon recede. Sixty days after this correspondence, prices began to fall rapidly. Jones was one of the big figures of the time, a splendid manufacturer, a good deal of a politician, having been chairman of the Republican National Committee, and an incurable "bull." I have previously spoken of his predictions but I will add that he had the faith to act on them and when in 1884 with everything booming, people suddenly quit buying, he was left with a vast quantity of high-priced steel on hand, and had it not been for the extraordinary financial resource of his firm, it would have been embarrassed.

Andrew Carnegie, on the contrary, although he also was an incurable optimist, always kept his business well in hand. He never speculated, and

when prices were dropping and all the steel manufacturers were faced with something that approached ruin he cut steel rails to $15 a ton,
arranged his production on a 24-hour basis, and
throughout all the dull time ran to capacity. He
told me that during this period, when many steel
concerns were losing money, he made as much
money as at any previous period of his business
history.

There was a general depression rather than a
panic in 1884. I do not recall any considerable
failures. There were a number of smaller ones
but no great and dramatic failures like that of Jay
Cooke. People simply got tired of rising prices
and quit buying, thereby to my mind showing
common sense. But to the mind of the man who
had stocked up recklessly in the expectation of
reckless buying at reckless prices, the country was
going to the dogs.

The farmers were particularly dissatisfied with
prices. They had been making money, but at the
low price to which farm products fell they declared
that they could not make a decent profit and would
not bother to increase their production. I have
always had a good part of my business directly
with farmers and in all these years, trading with
thousands of farmers, I have never heard one admit
that prices were satisfactory, and only one, in my
recollection, admit that he was making money. I
should regard a farmer who was not thoroughly

dissatisfied with prices and who was not declaring
that he ought to stop farming and cease putting out
crops to rot in the fields as an exception. I should
regard him as even more an exception if ever he did
fail to plant to capacity.

It is, of course, entirely impossible for the majority of farmers to know whether or not they are
making a profit. They keep at the best only cash
accounts and rarely have any way of ascertaining
costs. So no matter what are the prices they are
bound to be dissatisfied because all they spend,
whether personally or for the farm, whether charge-
able to expense or capital account, is regarded as
an expense. In the view of the average farmer a
net profit would be the sum left over after he had
made all the purchases he regarded as essential.
By that method of calculation a satisfactory profit
is impossible.

The farmers often discover by reading the farm
papers the large sums of money they are losing.
In every depression I have heard farmers speak
feelingly in terms of millions and billions of dollars
how much the farmer was losing, and they seemed
to regard themselves as vicariously losing these
vast amounts. As a matter of fact, in the average
farm a large portion of the product is consumed
upon the place and it does not make the slightest
difference what is the market price for this home-
consumed portion of the product. But I have
seldom been able to convince a farmer of this or

to convince him that if he received high prices for his products he would also have to pay high prices for other products.   Although I have a vast number of friends among farmers and am something of a farmer myself, I regard any attempt to satisfy the farmer either concerning the price he receives for his product or the price he must pay for what he buys, as being in the class with perpetual motion.

I have often tried to explain prices in bushels of wheat—to show that he paid me no more bushels of wheat than before and that often he paid me less, but this made little impression.

With business dropping off, we had cancellations of orders and were left with more stock on hand than we cared to have, but we immediately reduced expenses all along the line and started out at once to get rid of our merchandise—some at a small profit, some at no profit.   Because we made our reductions at once we were quickly able to clear our stockrooms and because we had little high-priced stock on hand we could take advantage of the lowering prices of raw material and sell our finished product at low prices but at a profit.   Holding on to higher-priced stocks in a depression in the hope of higher prices generally is bad business, for then one postpones the time when he can buy and sell in the usual relation to the price level of commodities.

The country was in a dissatisfied mood, which usually forecasts a change, and at the 1884 elections, Grover Cleveland, a Democrat, won out over his Republican opponent. An election held in the midst of a business depression generally brings a change of party in power. Failing all else, we always blame the Government for bad business and always the quacks come forward with sure remedies.

The quacks never are elected but they cause the party in power to be defeated. The opposition in this emergency has to nominate a conservative candidate and we have the odd spectacle of the radicals voting for a conservative rather than for the nominee of the party in power, no matter how liberal he may affect to be. Cleveland was a very solid, conservative man. And he proved a fine bulwark against the economic lunacy of the times.

These political changes seem always to proceed upon no higher foundation than a slogan. For instance slavery was often justified because it was "to the best interest of the improvident slave himself" and then, too, it was "more productive than free labour," and finally, as a clinching answer to any one who advocated the cause of liberty, came the Socratic question: "Do you want your daughter to marry a nigger?" The convictions behind these slogans, or engendered by them, were so fixed that as a political force they were defeated only by trial of battle—that is, by the Civil War. The Republicans conducted the Civil War, but Lincoln did not conduct it as a partisan war, for he brought into his councils and sent into important posts in the field leading men of the party that opposed him. But the war was under Republican administration and growing out of the war, the same party had on its hands the giving of a social status to the freed men and the reëstablishing of the national credit. These great questions were not set entirely at rest until 1880.

As late as that year the Republican victory appeared to most cool-minded business men necessary for the maintenance of specie resumption. Personally I have always been an Independent in politics voting for the party that I believed could best serve the country, so I have no prejudice whatsoever in discussing either party. I have voted for Republicans, Democrats, and Progressives.

The Republican Party in reëstablishing the credit of the country had found it necessary to advocate a large revenue and ample taxation. The victory in our civil conflict had been distinctly that of an industrial civilization over a feudal or patriarchal one. The great industrial enterprises were on the side under whose leadership the victory had been won, and naturally when their influence came to be active in their own behalf, it was the party to which they had attached themselves that most felt it. Pennsylvania, as our largest industrial community, has always been overwhelmingly Republican in national affairs and therefore it was a very easy journey for a party that had begun with the high moral purpose of preserving the Union to become a party advocating a high tariff. Thus arose what we know as the "American system of protection."

The Democrats found their power in the South. Being then a party of States' Rights, they opposed a tariff for other than revenue, in which position they were fundamentally no less selfish than the Republicans, for the rank and file of the Democrats would never have cared a rap about States Rights in relation to the tariff had it not been that the Southern states, being exporters of cotton and not then manufacturers, wanted to make their purchases in markets where the prices were not artificially raised by tariff restrictions.

There has never been any altruism in the whole tariff discussion. The tariff proceeds on a theory that it is not only desirable but also possible to reduce imports and yet leave exports undisturbed, and out of this arises the delusion of the favourable trade balance. Having the trade balance in our favour means that we export more than we import. We have discovered that, although a small balance in our favour may be liquidated in gold, a large balance must be liquidated in goods or not at all. It is not possible to increase the supply of any commodity in any market without lowering its exchange value, if there is nothing to excite and increase purchases. In the case of

gold we call this lowering "an increase in prices"
but the difference is in phrase and not in meaning.

The expense in gold of producing goods for export must continually increase as long as gold ex-
portations last, while the return for the goods not
only does not increase, but as our absorption of gold
creates a comparative scarcity in the countries that
send it, the return actually decreases.   The countries with the smaller gold stocks are thus able to
offer us their goods at smaller prices in gold expression while we through higher supply of gold
become more and more disposed to buy them.   So
that eventually these price differences overcome
the obstacles we set up to the importation of goods
and force imports again to equal exports.   As
Adam Smith says: "When you dam up a stream of
water, as soon as the dam is full as much water
must flow over the dam head as if there were no
dam at all."

It takes a surprisingly short while to fill the trade
dam.   This is not the place for a tariff discussion
(which I went into rather fully some years ago in a
book written in collaboration with my brother
Henry, entitled "Economic and Industrial Delu-
sions").   But I have not been able to discover,
during a rather careful study of our whole economic
history (and the personal experience of a good part
of it), any benefit which the country has ever de-
rived through import duties for other purposes than
revenue, excepting in the case of certain industries

which it seemed good for the country to have and yet which could not reasonably be expected to acquire the initial capital to make the start against world competition. If infant industries could begin with large capitalization they would not need protection, for they could finance themselves over the losing years, but it is not reasonable to expect that such a large amount of capital will be subscribed to a new venture and hence a tariff is sometimes valuable in permitting the experiment to be made on a smaller capital.

The product we manufacture has usually been protected, and my view as expressed some years ago and which I find no reason to change is this: "We manufacture machinery on which, to protect us within the United States, a duty is set. But this duty is like that placed on imported wheat, of no assistance whatever to the producer. For we send a large portion of our manufactures abroad; in the markets of South America, South Africa, and Australia we are compelled, and owing to advantages in labour and machinery are able, to compete with all other producers in the world without protection. I do not need to prove that since we can trade in those markets without special favours we have no need of them to keep our place in this. If we were circumstanced like the owners of copper mines, for instance, with a supply so firmly held in few hands that consumers were completely at our mercy, and able to sell our product year after year at what is received for it in London plus the duty on it, we might get some advantage from protection."

But we could get none without engaging in a legalized pillage of our fellow citizens. The cost to us of this merely nominal guerdon of legislation is higher prices on the raw material of every machine or implement we put on the market—hence fewer and smaller sales. Wages are not increased in buying power by a protective tariff. Many times I have seen manufacturers put on the stand in investigations and heard them depose in this fashion:

"I confess, I am selling my wares for higher prices than English makers ask. If I had to compete with the English unprotected, it would be necessary for me to pay my hands less than I am now paying. Otherwise I must close and leave them without employment."

All this is gravely set before the guileless labouring man and gaping rustic, who are expected to take it on its face value, without any allowance for the facts that even practical men are often deluded, and that almost any man is prone to put powerfully the side of a question on which he sees his own interests. His testimony may after all mean nothing more than that he does not know all he thinks he knows, or else that he is getting a pretty good thing by making his customers pay more than the worth of the goods. It is defective in

another way; for the reduction of expenses, that
freer trade would be certain to bring about, is not
suggested.   Many manufacturers would save more
in reduced cost of raw materials were import duties abolished than they would lose in reduced
price or reduced sale of product.

Little attention is called to the fact that a manufacturer is usually paying his hands the regular
market rate of wages.   Competition exerts its full
force on him in that way.   It may happen, in rare
instances, where there is an exceptionally large
profit on his product, that the employer will pay his
men more than he is obliged to pay.   The intelligent workman knows this.   Patrick replied to his
employer, we remember, when advised to vote
with the Republicans if he wanted better wages:
"And if you thought the Republicans were after
raising my wages, you would be voting for the
Dimmicrats yourself."   An employer engages in
business, of course, with the object of making
money, and his business to succeed must necessarily be governed by business principles and it is
hypocrisy for him to state that it is simply run for
the benefit of the community.   The theory of
wages based on the testimony of employers is
chiefly remarkable, therefore, for its glaring omis-
sions.

The wages in one trade depend on what is paid
in others; and that wages could not be lowered
generally by free trade across the frontier becomes

very clear when we remember the laws by which such trade is necessarily governed. Commerce between nations is interchange of product for product. If any specie passes in these transactions, it goes in obedience to a law of supply and demand that custom-houses cannot control, from the country in which it can at the time be procured with less effort than can some bulky commodity, to one where the difference is the other way. Specie thus distributes itself exactly as do other products of labour, and its function in settling balances does not affect the general truth that international commerce is barter.

Since every purchase of a foreign product is therefore a sale of one of our own products, since the interchange takes place only because we find the same labour more effective when put on the product sold than it would be if applied directly to the product bought, the action that foreign trade has upon labour is, in a general way, to increase its productive capacity. If a difference in the wages paid to labourers in two countries can be maintained with a small volume of trade between them, what change can be brought about by making the volume larger? Labour would thus become somewhat more productive in each of the two, the supply of it not increased, and the demand certainly not diminished in either.

My particular interest in these tariff matters just now comes from observing that a policy of high protection follows every depression and usually forms part of a prosperity-hindering programme to restrict production. At the very moment that foreign goods are barred from our markets, our manufacturers, instead of taking occasion to increase their productivity by the introduction of the best and most scientific methods, apply themselves diligently to the restriction of production through trade association or trust agreement to the end of getting more money for less work.

There are many ways of accomplishing this end. They can reduce production by agreement. This is, of course, an injury to the workman as well as to the consuming public. On the other hand they have a legitimate economic advantage in being able to reduce overhead expenses. Tariffs have been called the Mothers of Trusts, and this is true, since without tariff protection the combination or trust might be beneficial—at any rate its power of injury would be curtailed if not destroyed.

Restriction of production in spite of every sophistry which surrounds it, has its end in making the country poorer. It is precisely in line with hiring people not to compete with you—that is, engaging in a conspiracy against the welfare of the nation.

Scarcely had the Civil War closed when all of the politicians, irrespective of party, began to go after the soldier vote and now history is again repeating itself. I have always felt and still feel that this is a country worth fighting for—that the Government does not owe anything to any citizen in comparison with what all the citizens owe to the Government, for if the Government is anything it is only the expression of the will of the citizens. When the citizens are called upon to defend the Government and no distinction or exemption is made in this call for service, then such of these citizens as are called are exercising a privilege collateral to that of the franchise and they should no more expect to be rewarded for having been given that privilege than they should be paid to vote.

There is, of course, the exception of those who are injured in the service of the country and therefore liable, through disability, to become public charges. They should be supported by the community as a whole—that is, by the Federal Government—instead of by individuals.

But there can be no excuse for the wholesale pensions that were granted in increasing number after the Civil War or for the bonuses which threaten to take their place after the Great War. It is not that the soldiers demand these perquisites —it is always the politicians who stimulate the movement in the hope of thereby securing election.

After the Civil War both Democrats and Republicans vied with each other in offering financial inducements for the soldier vote and they kept on doing so until, as the years passed, the vote of the war veterans ceased to be important. A bid for the soldier vote is always put upon patriotic grounds notwithstanding the fact that payment is the negation of patriotism. A man cannot mix patriotism and money if he has the remotest idea of what patriotism is, but I have never heard the bid for the soldier vote either in the past or in the present expressed in the only way that it can be truly expressed, which is:

"I will give you money that does not belong to me if you will vote to put me in power and then keep quiet about what I do when I am there."

The tariff, decently dressed, was the Republican bid for special privilege. Fiat currency was the special privilege bid of the opponents. This was first expressed in greenbacks and then in free silver and with the passing of the years and in its free-silver form it gradually fastened itself on the Democratic Party. The argument was that a plentiful supply of money made for good business, and therefore, if only you had enough printing presses and got out enough money, you could not fail to have good business—although most people will admit that while a little whiskey may make a man frisky, a great deal of it will drop him into a heap.

It was not good business that the currency specialists were after. They wanted something for nothing. It has never been possible to convince the majority of the people that prices are purely relative; they will think of prices in dollars and not in buying power, and by juggling the currency they know they can get more dollars. Rarely does any one go far enough to realize that these dollars would not mean more buying power. When the cry for free silver was raised, as far as those who felicitously called themselves "the true friends of the white metal" were concerned, they were trying only to get the Government to buy all the silver that they produced at a fixed rate in relation to gold and thus avoid the annoyance of having fluctuating prices for their silver. Of course, the prices would have fluctuated, for the price of gold fluctuates, but that they did not know.

What they did know, however, was that if you could get, through the free coinage of silver, ten dollars for what otherwise you would have gotten only $8, then debts already incurred could be liquidated at a discount. The East loaned money and the West borrowed it. Currency ideas that leaned to the repudiation of debts on plausible grounds therefore found favour in the West. Of course, they did not look ahead to the fact that if you cheerfully pay off the money you borrow at a good discount, you may be in trouble when you next need money and try to borrow it.

We heard a good deal then about "bloated bondholders" and "Shylocks," and the plain inference was that although it was perfectly proper to borrow money it was highly dishonourable to lend it. This theory has, I think, remained unchanged to the present day.

The point I am trying to bring out of my experience with these national economic questions is that it is always popular to bring out a quack and shortsighted remedy and it is always unpopular to suggest that to-morrow will be another day. And that always behind these quack and immediate remedies put forward for the good of the people is a considerable special interest which, being also extremely nearsighted, thinks it can make a turn at the expense of the welfare of the country.

I have found that the best antidote for acute economic insanity is ownership of property. My favorite example is Otto Steininger. He was one of my first employees and was what was rare in those times—a rip-roaring anarchist. He insisted that all wealth came from the workers and therefore should go back to the workers. He was particularly bitter against his landlord and hardly a week went by that he did not announce that he had definitely decided that he would like to shoot the landlord the next time he came around for the rent. Finally I asked him smilingly after one of these outbursts:

"Why don't you buy your own house instead of shooting your landlord? Then you would not have to pay any rent. If you do shoot him you may get into trouble."

He did not think much of the idea apparently but in a day or two he asked me how he could buy the house. I answered:

"That house can be bought for $800. You are getting good wages. I will buy that house for you, take $4 a week out of your wages, and in less than four years you will have it paid for."

He went off again. The next time he came back it was with his wife. He said:

"We are going to buy that house but since we have no children you can take $10 instead of $4 a week out of my pay envelope."

I bought the house and then Otto's chief concern was to get it paid for, which he did in a little more than a year. There was another house next door to him. In a short while after he had paid for his first house, he sidled up to me and said:

"I can buy that house next door for a thousand dollars. Now that we have no rent to pay we are going along good. What would you think about me buying that?"

He bought that house and joined the hated landlord class. Some years later when it was reported that a band of strikers were advancing on York to shut all the factories, Otto rushed into my office at the head of an excited group of men from the shop yelling:

"Get us a lot of shotguns and we'll keep those fellows out of here. Those damned fools expect a man to work and save and then walk in here and take what he has got without paying for it."

And that, I think, is always the way to develop a conservative.

One of my old blacksmiths took another tack. He was a pretty good blacksmith but he did like the dramshop and to the best of my knowledge never missed getting drunk a single Saturday night during the thirty-odd years that he worked for me. On Monday he was never quite himself but by Tuesday he always was, which meant that he was one of the best blacksmiths in the place. He fell very ill and sent word that he would like to see me before he died.

I sat by his bedside for a while and recalled to him, not in a preaching way, but in the father-and-son manner, that we always then had among us, how he had come to me so many years before as a strong and healthy lad and how liquor had wrecked his constitution. He knew that I did not drink and probably he thought I was trying to draw a parallel between him on his deathbed and me, although many years older, in perfect health, for with a grin he pulled himself on his elbow and said:

"Yes, I know all about that, but just let me tell you that I have had more fun in my life than you would have in a hundred years!"

CHAPTER XIII

THE RISE OF BIG BUSINESS

DURING the period from 1870 to 1880, business, which had formerly been conducted by individuals or partnerships, began more and more to take corporate form. Before then when one spoke of buying stocks or bonds he meant railroad stocks or bonds, for there were practically no others. Then industrial securities began to appear, but it was many years before other than railway securities were regarded as safe investments.

In consonance with the trend of business, incorporation became easier. Most states passed laws permitting the issue of charters and letters patent to corporate associations practically as of course, after a compliance with certain statutory provisions, instead of, as previously, making it incumbent upon those desiring to associate themselves into a corporation to secure a special enabling act from the state legislature. I think the convenient organization of the railways was the example that led in the beginning to the use of the corporate form.

Because businesses were growing larger and

beginning to involve many interests, they found serious embarrassment in the interregnum and the locking up of finances which, unless especially provided against, were imposed by the decedents' laws of the states. Most of these industrial corporations as at first formed were really only partnerships with the stock very closely held and amounting to all intents and purposes, excepting from a legal standpoint, to no more than partners' interests. A little later it was discovered that additional money might be had without losing control by the issuance of bonds, and still later came the non-voting preferred-stock idea.

The preferred stock was devised by the longer-headed corporate organizers who saw that in the case of an industrial organization an issue of bonds always constituted a danger, for the interest had to be paid whether or not any profitable business was done. A company therefore was safer with the preferred-stock issue than with the bond issue, which, of course, generally involves a mortgage. But it was not until very recent years that astute investors began to appreciate that the preferred stock of a company without bond issues is sometimes a better security than would be a bond of the same company. It took a long time to get away from the real-estate-mortgage idea and to realize that an investor could in any event get a return only from what the corporation earned, and that a perfectly sound corporation might, by reason of a couple of bad years, be forced to borrow money to avoid a default in bond interest and thus invite a failure that would not have occurred if it had been permitted to husband its resources through the passing of stock dividends. For a foreclosure sale of a big property rarely fetches 100 per cent. cash. As a rule, however, the first mortgage bonds of good companies which have been in successful operation for some time and earned several times their interest charges are rightly regarded as safer investments than stocks. We incorporated our own business in 1889.

As lawyers and business men became more familiar with the form of corporate organization they began to use it for less legitimate purposes —for the avoidance of personal liability, and to make profits out of organization instead of out of operation. It was not at first realized by the general public, and perhaps it is not yet realized, that the issuance of a share of corporate stock of the par value of $100 does not make that stock worth $100 or worth anything beyond the earning power of the property it represents.

The great advantage of the corporate form was the opportunity that it gave for the acquisition of new partnership capital and we began then the economic progression to larger units of business. The small manufacturer rapidly gave way to the larger corporation. For instance, farm

implements such as wagons and ploughs and
harrows had been rather generally manufactured
by crossroads wheelwrights employing but one or
two hands. The larger manufacturer was able
to install machinery and to fabricate in what
was then considered quantity—although at no
time in the eighties or in fact until years afterward did we fully appreciate the value of repeti-
tive processes and the intricate sub-divisions of
labour which now distinguish our most efficient
industries.

What we did was to introduce more machinery
and to some extent specialize labour and even
this small beginning in efficient production was
amply sufficient to turn out a product so much
cheaper than that brought forth by individual
endeavour that the crossroads builders became
simply blacksmiths or repair men and not in-
frequently gave up their shops altogether and
hired out in the larger factories. Being used to
hard work and initiative, these men were usually
extremely valuable workers and a good proportion of the superintendents, foremen, and under-
foremen in the larger factories were men who had
previously been in business on their own account.

It was not until the nineties that the corporations
began to combine to any extent under trust agree-
ments and it was still later that the very large
combinations of corporations into "trusts" were
formed. I have always held that this progression

has been of the greatest possible benefit to the country because the tendency was to eliminate waste and, in spite of the attempts at monopoly or interference with competition, the real growth of the truly big corporation was due to the fact that it could manufacture and sell goods more cheaply than could the less efficient small producer. And the more goods we get at low prices the better off is the country.

In this larger view I consider it bad business to attempt to get orders away from another man unless you can give as much or more for the money than can he. The growth of the larger corporation directly affected our business some years later. We had been manufacturing harvesting machinery, but when the International Harvester Company came into the field with its own sawmills, furnaces, rolling mills, etc., to supply its raw material, and with its great organization it could give more for the money in harvesting machinery than could we, so I felt that it was necessary to discontinue such lines as the Harvester Company could make and sell more cheaply than I could.

Some years later, when the Harvester Company was sued under the Sherman Law, the counsel for the Government, knowing that I could not successfully compete with the big company in the manufacture of certain lines, called me as a witness for the prosecution. I readily testified my inability to compete and then I went on to say that I considered the Harvester Company as a public benefactor because, by reason of its organization, the farmer was able to buy a better article for the money than he was able to buy from me. In the midst of my testimony an attorney for the Government interrupted me angrily:

"I do not want to hear another word from that witness."

"I propose to speak the truth," I replied. "You should have followed the very good rule of knowing what your witness was going to testify to before you called him."

The Judge directed me to continue and I told the Court that I had always favoured any policy which gave the greatest good to the greatest number and I felt that I should accord honour and not malice to any man who, by better methods, successfully competed with me.

That rule has brought me business in ample volume and I have consistently followed it even to the point of taking the initiative and refusing an order when I knew the prospective buyer could get more for his money elsewhere. This is not only sound economics but good business.

For instance, some years ago a man came on from New York to place with me an order for a large number of cast-iron columns. I should have liked to take the job but I knew there was another factory in town especially equipped for the kind of work he wanted and that it could serve him to better advantage than could I. Therefore, instead of taking his order I referred him to my competitor. A few days later the competitor met me on the street and he said:

"I got that job. What in the dickens have you got up your sleeve? If I could not get a job myself I would be hanged if I should let any other man in town get it." I told him that, on the contrary, if I could not get a job for myself I should try to see that somebody else in town did get it. Fortunately, with the introduction of manufacturers' associations and chambers of commerce, this disposition has become general.

But suppose I had taken that job—and this is only one out of many cases—and the buyer had later discovered that I had not been frank with him? He would have had no legal cause for complaint and perhaps he would never have thought to complain, but should I have had his hearty good will and the assurance that he was safe in trading with me on an absolutely frank basis? One gets friends by being a friend and personally I have never been able to understand envy or malice. Why should not one be glad to see another get on? Why is it not a satisfaction to see any man honestly accumulate property and gain wealth? Why is it not pleasant to have a successful man build himself a handsome residence? I, standing outside, can have all the pleasure and appreciation of its beauty, while he, standing inside, has to pay the taxes!

The corporate form with its successions in management undoubtedly did tend to remove the employer from his men and brought about a gradual change in the character of the workmen. Undoubtedly it has brought a remarkable increase in machine efficiency, but I think man efficiency has decreased.

I have a number of men who have been with me more than fifty years and on the general average these men, all of whom are past sixty-five and some past seventy years old, do more in a day than the employees of the present generation. As one laughingly explained to me not long since:

"I have not yet learned the art of working slow."

Some of these men are remarkable characters. Take four who have been with me more that fifty-five years: George Witmer, who packs for export. He refuses to be bothered with packing lists; he knows what ought to go in each case, and I do not remember that he has ever made a mistake. Peter Rentzel is the head of the plough wood department in the export division and knows all there is to be known about that department, while Thomas Leader, a lumber inspector, can get more out of a plank of wood than it would seem possible that the plank contained. And Wesley Hildebrand, for many years foreman of the pattern shop, takes the same interest in his work and the success of the factory as though it were his own.

We lost, by death, a very remarkable man—almost a genius—in Henry Eisenhart. He assisted in developing and perfecting a number of patents, especially in threshing machinery, but he would never consent to take out any of these patents in his own name. He insisted that he was hired by the year, that therefore his time in or out of the shop belonged to me and that the results of whatever he did belonged to me. It was quite impossible for any one to get him to shift his position in this matter of patents. He was the foreman of the carpenter shop but really knew something of what was going on in all the shops. In addition to being a good workman he was also a good citizen and at one time they wanted to nominate him for mayor on a ticket that would have insured his election. He consulted me and I advised him that he would be happier as foreman than as mayor and so he unhesitatingly refused the nomination.

With the rise of corporations came the organization of labour, first in one form and then in another, although labour at no time was so extensively organized as under the American Federation of Labour during the Great War. We had its predecessor, the Knights of Labour, a somewhat radically inclined body that eventually wrecked itself by endeavouring to become a political body. I have never at any time found that the real workingman of this country when away from his job would consent to vote on a basis different from that of any other citizen of the Union.

I regard the human relation in industry as the most delicate part of the complex economic machine and, probably because it is so delicate and so easily disrupted, it receives more than its share of theories that are not based upon experience and which do not in practice work out. It was Aristotle who said: "It is safe to follow no theory that is not buttressed by practice." While theoretical discussion has great value, industrial relations, questions pertaining to capital and labour, particularly to the attitude of workingmen, can best be solved, it seems to me, by those who have united practice with science in forming conclusions.

Collective bargaining is one of the theories which sound well, but in practice it means that men who know nothing of your business, have no intimate personal touch with your workmen, come in and dictate as to the management of that business; in practice it makes it impossible for the management to employ good and efficient workmen who are needed unless those workmen are members of or will join the particular union controlling that shop. In practice it means that men in whose judgment and good intentions no intelligent person can for a moment have faith, seek to put what amounts to a throttle upon industry, for the ostensible benefit of the workingman, but in reality, in the majority of cases, for their own ulterior and destructive ends.

Again, we might also pertinently inquire how a bargain can be made when one side has neither legal nor moral responsibility, wants none, and only too often repudiates contracts when made. I have no quarrel with the unions. The right to organize for mutual protection and benefit is not questioned; neither is there any question but that through the instrumentality of unionism the workers in some cases have secured for themselves desirable and beneficial reforms which otherwise might not have come, or come only after long delay, having been grudgingly conceded under the pressure of competition by autocratic and unprogressive employers. Unionism's danger, however, is that of becoming autocratic itself. One of its principal objects appears to be, in all too many cases, that of getting a strangle hold upon an industry and then putting on the screws. On the part of the independent workman to whom unions are distasteful and who prefers to retain his liberty of action, the closed shop operates to shut the door of opportunity and deprive him of his primary and inalienable right to pursue his lawful vocation without interference.

The unions must eventually see that they are on the wrong track, and under the guidance of more enlightened leadership they may eventually become of real benefit to their membership and an important and beneficial part of the social organization. If the domination of extremists is encouraged or permitted, as now in many labour organizations, they invite disaster, not only to themselves but also to the industrial fabric generally. It has been always thus. No happiness or contentment can grow out of the seeds of envy and hatred. The condition of Russia furnishes a striking object lesson.

It is often said that the door of opportunity is shutting in the face of the wage earner. There could be no greater error. His opportunities for advancement are much greater now than they were when I commenced business; they were never so good in the history of the world as now and in this country. If he is only willing to pay the price of success, which involves economizing and doing his best, he will find the avenues open. There is no use blinking the fact that there are many whose limitations are such as to preclude their ever rising above a humble station. This is no discredit to them, and they are always entitled to just and fair treatment, but under no social arrangement holding any chance of permanence can it be expected that they should receive the same reward that comes to those of greater native ability who make full use of their talents.

I am persuaded that it is as idle for capital and

labour to fight as for the hands to fight the head. Both are absolutely essential, are interdependent, and I believe the working classes as well as the employing class will eventually come to understand this. A great deal depends upon management and personal contact. I could mention a number of examples. One of our foundry employees, a number of years ago when we were working on a large export order taken at a narrow margin, complained that he and some of his companions were not receiving sufficient pay in proportion to the rest. I knew they were getting all we could afford to pay, but referred him to the department heads with instructions to them to investigate the matter thoroughly and impartially and give him the result, after which I told him to come to see me, and if we could afford to pay more we should do it. As he failed to appear, I sent for him. When he came, he said:

"I am a good sport. I find you are paying all you can afford to pay, and am afraid if you changed our pay for that job you would have to reduce it." The investigation had proved that we could not afford an advance.

On another occasion, fifteen or twenty years ago when I had practically retired from active management, a large export order which was wanted in a hurry was dragging along, and the superintendent told me it was utterly impossible to get it out in time. I knew the men and told the superintendent to go off on a vacation—I would take care of the shop. He went, and I took charge, going out in the factory and joining with the men. They were spurred to renewed effort, largely increased their output, took the greatest interest in the game of beating time, and enjoyed it as much as I did myself. Needless to say the job was gotten out in the time promised.

There is a great deal in keeping in close contact with the workmen—in treating them as fellow workers. They should understand that they are working *with* the employer, rather than *for* him; that the employer's business is to provide them with work so that he can keep them continuously employed and pay their wages. If they are given a square deal, there will be no difficulty between employer and employed if they are not interfered with by outsiders.

I am fain to believe that the eventual result of the present unrest and discontent will be a better relation between capital and labour, employer and employed, than has ever been enjoyed before. It has set men to thinking and planning. There are many promising signs, and I believe the true prophet must be an optimist. It has been established in our plant. Meetings of foremen and managers are held weekly, as well as weekly meetings of an executive committee chosen by the men from amongst their fellows, which comes together in connection with the management for the discussion of improvements or complaints and the well-being of employees generally. The system has so far worked admirably. Even with the greatest care and fair dealing, however, a strike is always possible from outside interference. There is a great deal to be said in favour of the theory of profit sharing, letting wages depend entirely upon the profit, but if practised at the time this is written (August, 1921) the workmen would have nothing to live on—another proof that a theory must be buttressed by practice before it is safe to follow. Of course, I favour giving bonuses where there are extra profits.

The depression of 1884, as I have noted, caused the election of Grover Cleveland. I usually voted the Republican ticket and besides I had a personal affection for Blaine, the Republican nominee, and therefore I did not vote for Cleveland in his first campaign; but afterward I came to know Mr. Cleveland very well indeed and to esteem him as one of the greatest executives that this country has ever produced. I did not know him personally before election, although I had known him through friends and by correspondence, and was particularly impressed by his veto of the 5-cent-fare bill on the New York elevated railroads.

The franchise permitted the roads to charge a 10-cent fare and Mr. Cleveland, although he approved of the experiment of a 5-cent fare and believed it would pay under the conditions then prevailing, would not consent to making himself a party to breaking what he considered a state contract. A night or two after his veto he appeared in a New York theatre and the audience rose and hissed him. Yet they turned around later and elected him President. I was talking to Judge Black of this veto and he said to me:

"There is a remarkable man. He approves of the 5-cent fare and knows that it is popular and knows that signing the bill would have made him popular personally, but he vetoed it simply because it would be a clear breach of faith and he would rather antagonize every citizen in New York than break faith. That act is brave enough to make him President of the United States."

I called to see President Cleveland after his inauguration and he said to me:

"I feel simply overwhelmed with the responsibility of my position. I feel that I should like to shut myself up for a month and think over things and try to insure against mistakes. I am now President of the United States. I am no longer a party man, but believe that he serves his party best who serves his country best."

During his two terms I saw Mr. Cleveland many times and he used to discuss public affairs with me with the utmost freedom. I had especially interesting conferences with him during the several crises that marked his administrations.

It seems not to have been generally realized

that in January, 1895, this country was on the verge of financial ruin. The advocates of unlimited silver coinage had succeeded in so thoroughly alarming the world that foreigners were selling our securities. All of the free gold was being exported and both banks and individuals were hoarding. A canvass of the financial institutions demonstrated the impossibility of floating a bond issue upon satisfactory terms in gold or of using any other means to get together a sufficient stock of gold to save the Treasury. The situation was critical. I made a special journey to Washington and had a long talk with the President. I found that things were even worse than I had feared. He had before him a telegram from Mr. Jordan, the sub-Treasurer of New York, saying that at the present rate of depletion the gold balance would be exhausted within forty-eight hours.

The President explained to me that he had a plan to raise the money to tide over the Treasury until September 1st (when our trade balance ought to turn and give us a supply of gold) by selling bonds to J. Pierpont Morgan in connection with August Belmont, the agent of the Rothschilds, with the understanding that they would pay gold for the bonds. Mr. Cleveland said they had made a very satisfactory offer. He further said that since all United States bonds would unquestionably be paid in gold at maturity there was no reason why the new bonds should not be so worded, but Congress was opposed to the issue of gold bonds and therefore he had to act without their consent.

It was estimated that this issue made in Europe at the higher rate of interest, would cost the country over $10,000,000 more than if Congress had authorized the issue as at first proposed. I strongly advised the issue of sufficient bonds to stop the export of gold, but said that the plan would arouse great opposition in Congress. The President agreed with me.

"But," he assured me, "I propose to protect our gold reserve and the financial honour of the country regardless of criticism. While I am President there will be no suspension of gold payments."

The President carried out his plan. He issued the bonds and they were sold in Europe. On the very day of issue the gold loaded on vessels in New York for transport to Europe was taken off and returned to the banks and with the outflow of gold stopped business at once revived. The President had favoured a popular loan. He did not want anything else, but when he found that impossible, he resolutely availed himself of the next best thing in spite of criticism. Congress and not the President was responsible for the extra cost of the loan because of its issue without Congressional authorization, but since the business of the country was suffering to the extent of a million or more dollars a day (according to an editorial in the New York *Tribune*) by the uncertainty about the maintenance of the gold standard, this sum was recouped within two weeks. Cleveland was severely attacked by the New York *Tribune*, among other papers. I wrote the editor personally, enclosing their previous editorial and calling his attention to the fact that by their own calculation the amount had already been made up. His answer was that there would be no more criticisms of the President on that account.

I was at Woodley, the President's country residence near Washington, one Sunday afternoon, when some members of Congress came in and said:

"Mr. President, we wish to see you on an important matter." I got up, but he motioned me to keep my seat. They continued: "We have about decided to declare war against Spain over the Cuban question. Conditions are intolerable."

Mr. Cleveland drew himself up and said:

"There shall be no war with Spain over Cuba while I am President."

One of the members flushed up and said angrily:

"Mr. President, you seem to forget that the Constitution of the United States gives Congress the right to declare war."

He answered: "Yes, it also makes me Commander-in-Chief, and I will not mobilize the army. I happen to know that we can buy the island of Cuba from Spain for $150,000,000, and a war will cost vastly more than that and will entail another long list of pensioners."

I called to see Wayne McVeagh at this time to hear what he knew of the possibility of purchasing the island. We were good friends. He said:

"The President's statement is correct. We can buy that island and it would be an outrage to declare war."

Subsequently the *Maine* was destroyed. President McKinley felt the same way as Cleveland, but he could not stop the rush to war, although Spain may have had nothing to do with the destruction of the *Maine*.

President Cleveland's action at the time of the great Chicago strike was among the most noteworthy of his several large achievements. It will be remembered that Chicago was in a state of partial anarchy, the leader of the disorder being Eugene Debs, lately the Socialist candidate for President. Altgeld, the Governor of Illinois, seemed to be in sympathy with the strikers. There was apparently no ground for Federal interference until the United States mail was held up. The President requested Governor Altgeld to see that the mails were not interfered with. Altgeld replied in effect that the affairs of the State of Illinois were exclusively his own business. To this Cleveland replied summarily:

"I have ordered General Miles, accompanied

by United States troops, to see that the laws are obeyed and the mails not interfered with."

Everyone knows the result. The transportation of the mails was resumed and they have never been interfered with since. The President told me that he looked upon his action in this case as one of the best moves he had ever made.

"It established," he said, "in the minds of the people the fact that the mails of the United States could not be interfered with by any one."

During the McKinley-Bryan contest, some of my friends conceived the idea that I ought to be a sound money candidate and that I was well fitted for the place. A committee visited me. I had no idea of accepting but told them I would refer the matter to Mr. Cleveland, who was at Buzzard's Bay, and be guided by his advice. His reply was characteristic. He advised against a third party candidate. His letter to me was exceedingly friendly. I did not want the nomination or approve of a third party candidacy, and when the committee visited me, I felt very sure of what Mr. Cleveland would say.

Mr. Cleveland's efforts for tariff reform were among his great works. Although a Pennsylvania manufacturer and usually voting the Republican ticket, I have always been opposed to extreme protection as a breeder of war and father of monopolies. Mr. Cleveland's tariff reform message at the end of his first term was one of the best that ever came from the White House. As a matter of policy I was inclined to think that he should wait till after the election before sending it forward, and called to see him in regard to it. Mr. Dorshimer, connected with a New York paper, the *Star*, told me the purport of the forthcoming message at the Ebbitt House in Washington. He had seen the manuscript and so also had Don Cameron, Senator from Pennsylvania, who, by the way, was not fond at all of Harrison, and he had said that Cleveland was sure of election if the message were not issued. I went to see the President about it, told him what I had heard, withholding the source, as the message was given to me in confidence. He was surprised that I knew anything about it for, he said, only two or three people had supposedly seen it. He asked me why I disapproved. I said only because it ·might interfere with his reëlection, and he would have more time if elected to carry out the good work. He answered:

"I am surprised that you should take such ground." He asked whether I did not think the time was proper to issue the message—the people were much interested in the subject. I said: "Yes, except that it might defeat you."

He returned:

"We are enjoined not to do evil that good may come, or avoid doing good for fear that evil may come."

He referred me to his original letter of acceptance written when first nominated in which he took a stand against a second term for President on the ground that there was danger of its influencing the President's acts—and he added:

"I should stultify myself if I failed to let the message go forward from any fear that it might affect my election."

I, of course, could make no argument against that, and left admiring him, if possible, more than ever before. He was not elected that term, but he received the majority of the American vote and was chosen again at the succeeding presidential election.

CHAPTER XIV

FORGING AHEAD

IN EVERY important business depression, excepting the one which we are just now passing through *(1921) and which has involved the whole world, I have found the export side of my business to be little short of a godsend, and since the close of the Civil War I have tried to keep a rough average of one quarter of my output going overseas. The proportion has varied with the state of the home trade. The result has been that our factory comes rather close to holding a record for continuous operation.

We have rarely shut down or even gone on part time, at least until the recent depression, and this has enabled us to make very satisfactory annual profits without finding it necessary to take any undue profit on a single sale or the sales of a single season in order to cover the costs of some previous period of idleness. This has had a steadying effect upon our workers. As everyone knows, that which above all a worker fears is the loss of his job either through discharge or through a shutdown. Our workers, so long as they cared to work, have been practically assured of steady work and until

last year (and then only in one of the departments) we have never had labour trouble of any
kind. Our men have worked with us rather than
for us and even as the number grew large the
personal relation remained. Last year during the
period of general business lunacy when both proprietors and workers were endeavouring to discover
what the traffic would bear, a few of our newer
men, inflamed by an agitator, who told them that
they might have the moon for the asking, or words
to that effect, did strike for something or other and
remained out until they discovered that the moon
was not to be had for the asking. But aside from
this little emotional outburst we have had no difficulties and this long record of continuous profit
and continuously happy labour relation is, I think,
largely due to our record of continuous operation.

This continuous operation would not have been
possible without our overseas business. Several
times the export side has saved our commercial
record. I have already told how in the Panic of
1873 it enabled us to go on with but a two-day
shutdown. During the years from 1893 to 1897
when domestic trade was very dull indeed we lived
largely upon our export business. The weekly cash
receipts from our New York office usually covered
our payroll with something over and we went
through that most critical season not only without
curtailing our manufacturing but with a substantial increase.

The big thing to remember in the development of an export trade is the service that it performs during periods of dull domestic business. If things are quiet at home then prices and raw materials will be low and one is able to make especially attractive offerings for custom abroad. If, on the other hand, prices at home are high, then there is not so much opportunity successfully to sell abroad, but in the providential balance of things, selling abroad then becomes of little importance, for the prices at home would not be high if the market were not brisk. For these reasons I have always kept my export business in what might be called a take-it-or-leave-it condition. I have handled it through a separate firm known as A. B. Farquhar & Company, with an office in New York in which Cornelius Dunlea was my partner and general manager until his death, when I personally took charge of the entire firm although continuing the name. The export business in New York is now turned over to A. B. Farquhar Co., Ltd. Our idea has been never to load the export with any heavy fixed charge and thus we remain free to curtail or expand according to the home conditions. I am convinced that the American business man with a home market that comes close in purchasing power to equalling the markets of the rest of the world put together does best to keep the major portion of his business in that market, and use exports as a steadying influence. I have found it wisest, when we had plenty of orders at home, to pay less attention to foreign trade and then to expand again when the home market grew dull. This naturally involves an organization which is always in light marching order and prohibits the setting up of extensive branches or the incurring of heavy fixed charges of any kind. Of course, another business differently situated may find it advisable to make extensive plant and office investments in foreign countries. Large concerns, such as the Standard Oil, International Harvester, U. S. Steel, do find it profitable, but I think one does well rather carefully to ponder over whether the design is to go into foreign trade as well as domestic trade, or to supplement domestic trade with foreign trade. We are not in like case with the English or the Germans who have so little in the way of a home market. Their methods are by no means to be taken *in toto* as our methods.

The building of a foreign trade is usually looked upon as an undertaking calling for something more than an average amount of genius, but I have not found that it differs very much from the building of a domestic trade. I was drawn into it principally through my desire to know how other people lived. I had always been a student of world conditions, and always expect to be, and I have always liked to talk with people from abroad. The, perhaps old-fashioned, habit of falling into chats with fellow travellers on trains or ships is one that

I have liked and out of which I have gotten a
wonderful fund of information. I do not believe
that I ever met any one who did not tell me something that I wanted to know, and this information
is not only valuable in a human way—for first of
all we are human beings—but frequently proves
useful in a business way. I do not know how
many sales I have made through leads obtained
in casual conversation. It was this kind of talking
about among South American visitors that opened
up to me the possibilities of selling agricultural
implements in Mexico and South America. My
English catalogue was shortly followed by one in
Spanish.

This was some time after the Civil War and
we have issued a Spanish catalogue every year
since then. Some of these we sent directly to
names that I knew in the Americas and others
through the commission merchants in New York
and Boston. I have always favoured trading
through the commission merchants who buy for
cash and resell. This avoids the bother of credit
investigation and the expense of maintaining
agents. We have more or less followed this method,
although without formally committing ourselves to
it as a general policy. I am not in favour of any
policy in business that does not have a degree of
flexibility. We have at times hired agents, mostly
natives, and have sold directly to the local merchants. Being exclusively wholesalers, we do not

sell directly to the consumer. We have found it well always to retain sales agents who can conduct themselves anywhere and we have carefully investigated their reputations and responsibility before giving them power to commit us. Thus we to-day send out some of our goods through American commission houses receiving payment at the ship, and send out other goods to local merchants on whatever credit terms seem to be mutually satisfactory.

It is gratifying to know that our credit losses in foreign trade done through commission houses have been almost negligible. Our domestic credit losses have never been large but our foreign credit losses have been so small as scarcely to be worth speaking about. We, of course, at times have had to make extensions, and our customers have not always met their paper when it was due, but when they could not pay on time it was for some good reason and eventually they have paid. This is due, I think, to rather extensive inquiries that we make before giving credit.

The first direct foreign shipment that I recall was a lot of plough parts to South Africa about 1866. One of the first shipments of complete implements was to Paysandú, Uruguay, about 1870, and consisted of a number of ploughs that left on a sailing vessel owned by A. B. Morton & Sons of Baltimore. Most of these early South American orders went on sailing ships and since the sailings were few and far between, sometimes we had very narrow margins between the receipt of the order and the sailing of the ship. I remember particularly a car-load order due to go on a ship from Baltimore. Two days before sailing the order was complete with the exception of some fifty or sixty ploughshares which through an error had been delayed in the foundry. Ordinarily these remaining parts would have taken several days to finish. I got the men in earlier than usual on the next day, poured the shares with the first iron, milled them, and after six o'clock that evening, with the help of two of my men, personally packed them and took them to the car. The dispatcher, Hamilton Jamison, had gone, but we hunted him up and explained the emergency. He entered into the spirit of the thing.

"The fast freight goes down at eight o'clock," he said. "I will get that car through."

I took a train at about four the next morning, and, reaching Baltimore, went to Jackson's wharf and found that my car had not only arrived but had already been unloaded and the vessel gone. Delays are bad enough in domestic business; in overseas business they are fatal because, if you miss a ship, the goods may miss the season during which they were expected to be sold.

It has been said that I was one of the first Americans to export agricultural implements. In 1870 we had a good-sized order from the Ames Plough Company of Boston for South Africa, which introduced our products in that section of the world, and I have always done a good deal of business in South Africa. The South Africans had mostly bought English agricultural machinery but I have not found anywhere any tendency to discriminate in favour of the mother country. People anywhere in the world will buy American goods in preference to any other kind provided those goods give the best value for the dollar—which includes having them exactly suited to the purposes. There has never been and never can be, until human nature greatly changes, a discrimination against an article because of its place of manufacture. Campaigns in favour of home-made products are being gotten up from time to time all over the world, but nobody ever pays much attention to them unless the home-made article happens to be better and cheaper, in which case it would be bought without any campaign. Those who violently try to force the buying of only home-produced goods are usually those who have no need or intention of buying. The man who is actually going to buy gives lip service to all of these patriotic movements and then goes round the corner and buys according to the value of his dollar. I have found the English to be very fair competitors in South Africa and have had no difficulty in underselling them whenever I tried.

In 1884, while I was in England, Justin M'Carthy gave me a letter of introduction to Mr. Howard, head of the Howard Agricultural Implement Company, Ltd., and a member of Parliament, who was one of the larger manufacturers. They showed me through the works and I was particularly interested in what they called Plough No. 75 designed for South Africa. We discussed costs freely. They did much of their work by hand; I did most of my work by machinery. I found that they got their metal cheaper than I could get it but that my machinery made our fabrication cheaper and that my total cost was less than theirs. This I proved years later when after the Boer War the English Government opened bids for 20,000 of the No. 75 ploughs for South Africa. I won the contract at a lower price than they could be furnished by the English makers, and yet made a fair profit.

In 1873 during the home depression I pushed my export business and sold very extensively in South Africa, in Cuba, in Mexico, in Brazil, and in the Argentine. We have also sold since then in Russia and to some extent in Bulgaria, in Serbia, in Greece, and in Turkey. In fact, over the years our machinery has gone into nearly every arable part of the globe. Most of it has gone with our name on it, but wherever a local house or a commission merchant preferred to have the stencil or the name-plate omitted, we have omitted it without question. Naturally we like to have the advertisement of our name, but a buyer who is thoroughly satisfied will go to some trouble to ferret out the maker of what he has found to be a good article and we have received about as many re-orders from the sections where our goods were sold unmarked as from the sections where they were sold marked. I have always held that if you do your work to the very best of your knowledge and skill your product will have distinction whether or not your name is on it, and people will search you out to get more of the same. Of course we never made any distinction in quality between marked and unmarked products. When our work has been anonymous it has been through the desire of the purchaser and not through any desire on our part to put out less than the best.

The Russian trade is interesting. They are most extraordinary people and any one selling to a Russian must use meticulous care as to specifications. The first steam boiler that we sent there was rejected. I could not understand why, excepting that they claimed it was not according to specifications. I found that we had varied the specifiations; we had put in one more square foot of heating surface than had been called for! To the Russian mind it made no difference whether the heating surface was one foot over or ten feet under. They had ordered an exact article and that they had to have. They were not concerned with operation or utility or anything of the sort. They were immersed in specifications. There is nothing quite so dear to the heart of a Russian as a long and intricate discussion over something that is of no consequence. In this respect they mentally belong to the Middle Ages. They love progress as they love the devil. We sent a shipment of ploughs to Russia in 1878. After waiting many months I wrote to discover what service they were giving, and some months later had a letter informing me that the ploughs had reached their destination ahead of the soldiers that had been detailed to guard them and the peasants, fearing that the ploughs were going to make less work, had held something in the nature of a pogrom and destroyed the whole shipment. They were paid for by the purchaser, however, as was also the boiler which had the extra foot of heating surface.

I have found the Russian peasant and the Russian workman to be pleasant, childlike fellows, but with very little of what we should call common sense and a most unusual capacity for believing anything that is patently untrue. I am not in the least surprised that they have permitted themselves to become the tools of the Bolsheviki. The Soviet form of government must be immensely appealing for it gives an infinite opportunity for talk and, as far as the peasants and workers are concerned, Communism cannot mean anything, for I never discovered any ambition on their part to own other than the most absolute and primitive necessities of life. The chapter on American trade with Russia will have to remain suspended until the mass of the Russians find Communism less amusing. They will enjoy Communism as long as it is a novelty—as long as they can talk. When it ceases to be a novelty; when they discover, as they are now discovering, that a diet of words is not sustaining, and that they have been imposed upon, then these half-blind hordes will run amuck as they did at the time of the Revolution. When they have quieted down, the Communists will have ceased to exist. I fear that the next Russian revolution will be very terrible and bloody. In the meantime there is little possibility of trade with Russia.

Mexico has always bought rather liberally from us and we began there in the early seventies mainly through the house of Braniff & Company, the senior member of which firm built the railroad from Mexico City to Vera Cruz and was a personal friend of President Diaz. I never travelled through Mexico exclusively on business—in fact, I have seldom travelled anywhere outside of the United States solely on business. My travels have been largely in the public service, although on these trips I have naturally been entertained by our agents or merchants. And I have kept my business eye open. I made rather an extensive trip through Mexico with the American Public Health Association, of which body I was one of the founders. This was in the time of President Diaz and he was particularly nice to us, entertaining us in his country palace as well as in the city.

He reminded me, in spite of the fact that he was

two thirds Indian, a good deal of Colonel Roose-velt. He was impulsive, had a rugged determina-tion, and a very wide general knowledge, not only of everything that went on in Mexico, but in the world. His English, however, was very weak and he disliked speaking in other than Spanish. He was an autocrat. There is no doubt about that. For instance, in Guanajuato I noticed a crowd around the State House and I asked a Mexican friend what it was all about. He said he did not know but he would investigate. In a little while he came back laughing, and said:

"The *rurales* have surrounded the State House under instructions not to let any of the delegates out until they vote for the man whom President Diaz had suggested as Governor of the province."

But they were scrupulous only as to the forms of observing the methods of democracy!

Our Public Health Association found much to admire, but criticized some unsanitary features in Mexico City. When we returned from our trip to Vera Cruz our attention was called to the fact that by order of President Diaz these unsanitary houses had been burned down.

A general proudly told me that in the interests of sanitation he had just burned down a great number of houses. He explained to me what an improve-ment it was to be rid of such a filthy quarter.

"But," I asked, "what did the people say who were living in those houses?"

"What did they say?" he mused. "Why, what do they say when it rains?"

I went out to the hacienda of Oscar Braniff, the junior member of the firm. He had a magnificent place extending over many miles. One of his overseers came in and reported:

"I have just made a fine haul for you, Señor Braniff. I have taken a lot of cattle, horses, and pigs from a portion of the hacienda about twenty miles away."

I did not quite understand this method of gaining livestock and began to ask questions. It came out that this portion of the hacienda was on the Braniff property which fact they had just discovered although people had been living there for generations farming the land and raising cattle and horses. The overseer had simply gone down and driven the occupants away. It did seem a high-handed proceeding and I asked Señor Braniff what would become of the squatters.

"Oh," he answered carelessly, "they will probably wander off and join some roving band." To his credit I may say he admitted that this system was all wrong and should be corrected.

Diaz's rule was firm. Mexico was an orderly community. He told me a young girl might then have safely travelled alone over the entire city. He did an enormous amount for the country. The best penitentiary I ever saw was in Mexico. I visited it with Mrs. Lopez, the wife of the Secretary of State. The institution was immaculately clean, the floors were all cement, and the convicts were dressed in clean, white clothing. They had work of various kinds, and in the evening attended school. The superintendent told me that he frequently let them out on honour to attend a funeral or marriage of a relative, and that invariably they returned on the date promised. Mexico was well-managed, but the masses had no opportunity whatsoever for promotion and incidents like that on the Braniff hacienda were far too common. They drove people out ruthlessly and they did not seem to care how many bandits rose up for, of course, these people were bound to be embittered and to turn bandit.

A Mexican becomes a bandit and then stops being one with somewhat less reflection than an American worker takes or leaves a job. It is simply among the occupations of the country and seems singularly unconnected with dishonesty. I have never found the Mexican to be especially dishonest—that is, to violate his pledge. He seems to have a very high regard for a certain kind of honour. But he is technical. You may with perfect safety hand him a banknote and ask him to have it changed for you. He will bring back that money to you at the risk of his life but, having safely delivered the money, he might not hesitate to shoot you a few hours later and take the money away from you. That, apparently, is a different transaction!

They are backward and they are more idle than it seems possible for a human being to be. I sent some American workers down with a shipment of machinery. They hired Mexican assistants and paid them 13 cents gold (about 25 cents Mexican), which they were used to receiving, but feeling that this was not enough they advanced to 25 cents gold, which was about 50 cents Mexican. Our people thought that this was only decent but they quickly found that they could not get more than three days' work a week out of any man, for three days gave the income that they had been accustomed to earn in six. We had to reduce the wages in order to get the work done. The exceptionally thrifty Mexican may wish to keep a month ahead, but the average Mexican of the lower class usually regards three days ahead as quite sufficient provision for his daily necessities. But they are not stupid. Our people find them clever in putting together machinery and they seem to hold on to every scrap of knowledge that they gain. In fact, if you get a Mexican interested in the study of anything he will go on most industriously. They simply do not, however, have needs that require much money and not having the needs they will not work for the money. Perhaps, after all, they are not as foolish as they seem to be. They simply have a different viewpoint and we are all entitled to our viewpoints.

Cuba also has been an excellent customer although not originally receptive to modern ideas. I canvassed Cuba in person many years ago taking our agent, who also acted as interpreter, with me. I found many farms being ploughed with bits of iron fastened to forked sticks and the methods of cultivation generally had not advanced much over those of ancient Egypt. I tried to demonstrate to one of these native farmers the advantage of our improved plough over his forked stick but he said that his father and grandfather had used what he was using and he would not insult their memory by making a change. However, there is a very considerable market in Cuba and it is constantly increasing.

South America proper is a field that most Americans have talked a great deal about and have neglected. We have always had a good business through South America and have many firm friends, particularly in Brazil and in Buenos Aires. I have personally nothing to complain of, but generally speaking I find that Americans are not sufficiently careful of the sensibilities of the South Americans. They resent bitterly our patronizing attitude and are very sensitive to the loud and boisterous manner of many of our travellers. Most of them do not like our assertion of the Monroe Doctrine—they think it meddlesome. In short, they do not like us, and in addition they envy us, which makes the situation all the worse.

And we have done almost nothing to change this

attitude. We have gone rather on the basis that South America is a vague continent in a way appurtenant to the only real thing in the Western Hemisphere—that is, the United States—and that it is inhabited by aborigines whose friendship and whose trade are not specially worth cultivating. Every North American business man visiting Buenos Aires and Rio Janeiro for the first time gets a distinct shock; he is really surprised to learn that these cities are as fine as any in the world. The same is more or less true of most of the leading cities of the Southern continent. They are a very different people from ourselves. The races are mixed, they are more European than we are, and have rather a European civilization super-imposed upon native customs than a really distinct civilization such as we have. The South Americans are quite as ignorant of us as we are of them. They have but a hazy idea of our power and of our size, and think of us merely as bumptious. During the last twenty years with the Pan-American meetings and the establishing of branch banks and closer commercial relations, the leading business men below the equator have learned to know more of us and we have learned to know more of them, and I think we are on the way to a much better relation. But it is one that it should not be necessary to urge, for there is great profit as well as much delightful intercourse to be had in a closer union. Generally speaking, South America does not require anything very different from what our home trade requires and they learn very easily and very quickly to use our machinery.

Much of our machinery is sent "knocked down" on account of transportation difficulties. South America is backward on railways. In many cases where the goods have to be taken over the mountains, the limit of weight for each package is 125 pounds and since they are carried on mule back we sometimes have had to send a boiler in such small parts that they could not even be riveted, yet the native labour satisfactorily put the boiler and engine together. The question of packing is one which many of our people strangely enough regard as of little importance. It is very important indeed to pack according to the conditions of transportation and to pack so securely that no harm can come to the goods *en route*. Yet many excellent American articles have gotten a bad name simply because they were so carelessly packed that they arrived in a damaged condition.

In Japan we have never done any large amount of business. The business done there has been satisfactory, however, as far as payments are concerned. In 1876 I sold a rice-thresher there; in the next year I wrote asking whether it had given satisfaction and they replied that it had given such entire satisfaction that they had adopted the design and were making it themselves! The Japanese have a way of shopping that is not unlike that of our dressmakers. They shop for designs to copy rather than for articles to use.

There is nothing particularly dramatic in the establishment of our foreign business. It has been a growth through the years. We have tried to make the best possible article and sell it fairly, treating the foreigner quite as though he were living in the next town instead of some thousands of miles away. He has usually liked our work and when he wanted something of a special nature, has sent on a sample for us to work from. We have made many orders from samples. The main thing is to sell the people what they want—but that is largely the secret also of domestic business!

CHAPTER XV

WHAT I HAVE LEARNED

SOMETIMES I am asked whether to-day we have as many great men as we had in times past and whether the comparatively few national figures to-day—men such as Judge Gary and Charles M. Schwab—are as big as some of the older figures. We have not as many nationally known men as we used to have, but I can unhesitatingly say that the reason for this is that the general average of men both in business and in politics is to-day immeasurably higher than ever it was. Some of the men in the past would have stood out under any circumstances, but it is to be remembered that fifty years ago this was not nearly so big a country and a man did not then need such great ability as he does to-day in order to be notable.

It is hard to make a comparison because of the change in conditions. For instance, Abraham Lincoln was a man who would have been remarkable anywhere, yet he was a child of the times and I greatly doubt if to-day he would ever have had the opportunity to become President and to become so distinguished. Of course, that is mere specula-

tion. But I do know that not a few of the politicians of former times could not exist in public life
to-day. For instance, take Daniel Webster. I
met him first through W. W. Corcoran.

Corcoran, who founded the banking firm of
Corcoran & Riggs, which afterwards became the
Riggs National Bank of Washington, was one of
the large figures of the Capital. At that time the
difference between the banker or business man and
the politician was very wide indeed. A member of
Congress was usually a lawyer and he looked upon
business as something rather lowly which was not
at all necessary to understand and which he rarely
did understand. They have not quite recovered
from that habit of mind! When a boy of about
twelve I met Mr. Corcoran rather oddly. Stroll-
ing along a street in Georgetown (now part of
Washington) I heard someone playing *Cujus Ani-
mam* from the *Stabat Mater*—rendering it magnifi-
cently. I stopped for a while and then, the door
being open, walked in and sat down. The player
was a girl of sixteen or seventeen. (Walking into
peoples' houses unannounced was not so unusual
in those days and especially in the South. I have
already told how once in a Southern mansion,
arriving late at the home of people whom I knew
only by correspondence, but who had invited me
to visit them, I was told by the major-domo simply
to walk in, hunt out an empty room, and occupy it).

The girl was not in the least surprised. She

asked me if I liked her playing, and I said I did, and she gave me the *Stabat Mater* selection again.   The room was hung with paintings.   We got to talking about them.   She told me they were copies of the originals hanging in the home of Mr. Corcoran, who long afterward founded the Corcoran Gallery. I wanted to see the originals.   She said her father was cashier in the Corcoran Bank and she could go to the Corcoran home any time she liked.   She took me to see the paintings and then took me down to introduce me to her father at the bank because I also wanted to meet Mr. Corcoran.   Corcoran was one of those men who turned anything he touched into gold.   He had made a great deal by buying land in Washington at a very low price.   He was a keen, shrewd banker and wielded a large if not always evident power.   He was one of the big men of the country.   We found her father, Mr. Hyde, in animated conversation with Mr. Corcoran. Daniel Webster had just been in to borrow money and Hyde had given it to him.

"Senator Webster asked me," said Mr. Hyde, "to discount his note for $100.   I told him we did not usually lend on a note unless endorsed, so he went out and brought in a note for $200 endorsed by another Senator, who had endorsed with the understanding that they should divide the proceeds.   I gave him the money."

Mr. Corcoran remarked that the only value of the note was as a curiosity—it would never be paid.

I afterward heard that the note never was paid and that the Riggs Bank still has it. Corcoran laughed about it but Mr. Hyde was worried. It seemed strange to me that the joint note of two United States Senators would not be worth $200, but United States Senators in those days could not be expected to bother themselves about little things like paying bills. The eloquence of Congress has decreased but its ordinary common sense and commercial integrity have increased. It is hardly likely you would find two Senators now failing to pay a joint note of $200.

Daniel Webster was very careless about all of his personal affairs. He was said to be scrupulous about paying his gambling debts but he did not bother with little bills. He often thought it quite enough to give a creditor a copy of his signature without bothering to honour the promise to pay ahead of it.

He was such a powerful, leonine sort of a man and his voice was so glorious and magnificent that I do not believe any one in the country would have ventured to mention such a trivial thing as money in his presence. Few more impressive men have ever lived—in fact, he had been called a living lie because, as was said, "no man could possibly be as great as Webster looked."

He was exceedingly clever. Everyone knows about his gift of oratory but in addition to that he was versatile. His mind moved like lightning. A lawyer friend told me of a case he tried against Webster in a New Jersey court. In those days the speeches to the jury more frequently decided the case than now. Webster came into court to address the jury quite a little the worse for wear. He had been profoundly investigating the effects of wine, which was a habit that not a few of our leading figures indulged in. His voice was good, his manner was good, but as he started to address the jury he unfortunately forgot which side he was on and with surpassing eloquence presented my friend's side instead of his own. His associates when they found what was going on kept pulling at his coat tails and making signals, but to no end. Once launched into an address nothing could interrupt Webster.

As he closed and started to sit down one of his colleagues gave him a particularly vicious poke and then all at once Webster remembered what he had done and without so much as cracking a smile he turned to the jury and said:

"Now, gentlemen, I think I have said and I think you will admit that I have well said, everything that can be said for the other side of this case. Now I shall proceed to show you that there is nothing in it."

And then he demolished the case he had built up. Webster was a genius, there is no doubt about that, but he would not fit into present-day conditions. And then there was Henry Clay who was of the same style. I met Clay several times and heard him speak. On one occasion my father persuaded a Democratic friend to go with him to a barbecue to hear Clay speak. It was customary then to roast an ox whole at a political gathering. He protested that he would not go to hear a damned old Whig speak, but at last was prevailed upon. Father mentioned to Clay that he had brought a friend along after some persuasion, and wanted to introduce him. Clay glanced at the man now and then during the course of his address, and by the time he was through had him waving his hat and cheering. When Clay came down from the platform he shook the hand of my father's companion who had been completely mesmerized, and who told him he was going to vote for him. Clay had a wonderfully magnetic personality. I once walked eighteen miles to Washington to hear him. I have always been fond of cross-country walking, and that time I took a straight course through the fields. I recollect passing a house where they had several fierce dogs who rushed out as though to tear me to pieces. A woman called for me to run. I called back that I was not afraid of dogs, and as they came up they commenced to wag their tails and jump up to my shoulder. I never was afraid of dogs, and they always seem to be fond of me. I never saw a dog in my life that would molest me if he came close.

But to get back to business. In 1889 I decided

to become a limited partnership under the name of A. B. Farquhar Co., Limited. We had been known before as "The Pennsylvania Agricultural Works," with my name as proprietor. The object of incorporation was to facilitate the distribution of my estate and also to give my sons, whom I expected to succeed me, some present interest in the business; and the advantage of the limited partnership over the regular corporation was that I was not obliged to have agents in all the different states in order to sue or be sued. I did not, of course, wish to relieve myself personally of any responsibility. I conservatively capitalized at but $500,000, although the real estate and property were worth considerably more, aside from all goodwill, patents, and the like. I made no change in the manner of conducting the business.

My daily routine was from seven in the morning until six in the evening, or later if any emergency required it. I was always on hand when the whistle blew, and began the day with a walk through the factory and a chat with the foremen and the men also. Until the management was turned over to my son some years ago I always kept in touch with everything that was going on, both in the factory and outside. Stenographers came in vogue about then and I was able to answer most of the letters that were received. We had no regular travelling men and did our business by circulars, advertising, and at my office desk. Most of the sales were made by correspondence, but many customers came to the factory. We also had agents, who sold the goods and assumed responsibility for the payment of customers' notes.

Trade was very dull from 1893 to 1897 and as I have before said we relied largely upon our export business to keep going. We took advantage of the dull years, as always, to improve our plant and machinery and to devise methods for getting out work at a lower cost. It has been my policy to take advantage of an extremely dull season to make improvements, for then materials may be bought at the bottom and also whatever outside labour is required can be had at a low price. It was my policy never to put up anything at the height of a boom or enlarge during boom periods. We have thus been able to keep the book value of our buildings far below what they would ordinarily cost. I have supervised the erection of all our factory buildings and the work has been done largely by our own men. This has served to keep our force intact and I think it is a good thing to be able, even though the idea may be old-fashioned, to change over men to new and unusual work rather than discharge them. Also it adds an indefinable something to men to work in buildings they have themselves erected. We have been able to do everything but the bricklaying and my old co-worker, Henry Eisenhart, was our main reliance. That man could do anything in the way of construction. He was one of the most versatile men I have ever known.

The presidential election is always a disturbing factor in business, but the depression of 1892, which resulted from other causes, was made less disturbing, because of the well-known conservatism and ability of Grover Cleveland. The country felt sure of a safe president no matter who was elected. There were labour troubles in 1892— especially the Homestead riot.

This riot never would have occurred had Mr. Carnegie been at home. There were also switchmen's strikes and a strike among the coal miners, showing a growing restlessness. These labour troubles were partly accountable for the depression in business of 1893. The troubles continued, but there was no financial panic until 1893, and there would have been none then, had we had the present Federal Reserve System.

In 1892 Governor Pattison appointed me a commissioner to the Columbian Exposition in Chicago and I was afterward made executive commissioner with practically the entire charge of Pennsylvania's participation in the Exposition. I had previously spent two months in Europe in the interest of the Exposition by appointment of the Secretary of State. This absence in Chicago was the first time I had ever been for any considerable period away from my desk. My eldest son, W. E. Farquhar, was superintendent and

W. A. Maigne was head of the sales department, and they managed affairs very well indeed although I kept in touch with them daily by telephone, telegraph, and mail. I did not believe in getting very far away from business at any time.

On the first of May, 1893, the great Columbian Exposition was formally opened to the public by President Cleveland. I accompanied him to the platform when he made the opening address, which, by the way, was admirable in tone and substance and was well received. It was made without notes. He was the only president who ever made an inaugural address without a note in his hands. The Chicago Exposition was a world event; there has never been anything to equal it in beauty before or since. Burnham, the great landscape architect, accomplished wonders. What was formerly a barren plain, without shrubbery or trees, he made rich with verdure almost overnight, moving large trees bodily and putting them in place as though they had grown there. The World's Fair was admirably managed by Harlow N. Higinbotham and a council of administration, headed by Judge Massey, Chief Counsel of the Pennsylvania Railroad. At a general meeting of the Executive Commissioners of all the states, I was elected president of the Executive Commissioners on the first ballot, which office I held till the close of the Exposition.

Harlow Higinbotham was one of the men whom

the country could well have afforded to know better. He was the practical manager of the whole Exposition and I think the secret of his management there as well as his remarkable rise in the Marshall Field store was an almost uncanny ability to estimate the character of men. He knew how to pick out men who were honest and reliable and who would do their work. I have always felt flattered that he believed in me. I had frequent opportunity to judge this ability to appraise character. Marshall Field had taken him as a boy because once while driving out through a country district and asking about certain customers, he was referred to young Harlow Higinbotham, who was then ploughing a field, as the one person in the neighbourhood who knew all about everyone. That is why Mr. Field hired him away from his father and that is why he so quickly became the credit manager of Marshall Field & Co. and eventually a partner.

After talking five minutes with a man Mr. Higinbotham, asking few questions and keeping the conversation seemingly casual, would know exactly how far he could trust that man—he would know not only whether he was deserving of credit but how much credit he ought to have. I remember one quite embarrassing incident. An East Indian came to the fair in charge of an exhibit. Mr. Higinbotham met him and then flatly refused to have anything further to do with him. He would not permit him to exhibit. I asked him why and he simply said most decisively:

"He is no good, I know he is no good, and it does not pay to trust a scoundrel. That man is a scoundrel."

A very handsome woman—a princess, I believe—was in the Indian party and she appealed to me. We together went to Mr. Higinbotham and asked what in the world we should do about the exhibit. He was as a rock about the appointed commissioner but he suggested to the princess that she take charge. There was no other way out. She did take charge. A little while later the man who had been appointed and who was absolutely unknown to Mr. Higinbotham—he knew nothing about him when he turned him down—decamped with all the jewels of the princess.

At another time in his office when I was present, a man came in to tell him that his mortgage was about to be foreclosed. He said his property was worth three times as much as the mortgage but he could not raise the ready money. That was during the depression of 1893. Mr. Higinbotham heard him out and dismissing him said:

"All right, I shall attend to that. Your mortgage will not be foreclosed."

"Do you know anything about that man?" I asked him.

"No," he answered, "excepting that I know he is telling the truth. He will pay if he can and I will tell the holder of that mortgage that I will be personally responsible."

I learned afterward that Mr. Higinbotham had saved the man from ruin, and that he did pay. I sat with Mr. Higinbotham some years later on the insurance investigation. A witness told a long and circumstantial story which was apparently accurate. The counsel for the committee turned to Mr. Higinbotham and asked:

"Is that man telling the truth?"

"I know that he is not telling the truth," said Mr. Higinbotham.

Then our counsel, Mr. Samuel Untermyer, accused the witness of perjury. The witness broke down and told an entirely different story.

During all of this time the country was having labour trouble. A man by the name of Coxey started a movement in Massillon, Ohio, for a great parade of the unemployed from all over the country to Washington. The intent was to influence Congress to do something or other, but exactly what nobody, not even the paraders, knew. Various detachments of what came to be known as "Coxey's Army" organized through the country. Some of them were unemployed workmen but most of them were men of anarchistic tendencies or the professional tramps who thought the trip would be good fun. The news of the army filled the newspapers and it actually, after many vicissitudes, did reach Washington although in somewhat battered condition. The Government, however, was ready and dispersed it without much ceremony. The march did not accomplish anything because there was nothing it could accomplish. It was a crazy idea but no crazier than the Bolshevism of to-day. There has never been a time when it has been impossible to organize the malcontents. I am beginning to think we should not be normal without them.

The labour troubles continued into 1894 when there was a great strike at the Pullman Works in Chicago of which I have already spoken.

There was a great deal of tariff discussion through 1894. The President favoured more liberal laws on foreign trade than Congress was willing to establish. The final outcome was the "Wilson-Gorman" tariff, which President Cleveland termed a tariff of "perfidy and dishonour," and would not sign. It became a law without his signature. He did not veto it because it was some improvement on the previous law.

During 1894 attacks on large corporations or trusts under the Sherman Law became popular, and there were proceedings against the sugar trust and the Standard Oil trust. Labour troubles continued, the most important being the strike of railway employees in Brooklyn, which was marked by violence and which required calling the militia to maintain order.

Among the men I knew during this period was

Wu Ting-Fang, Chinese Minister to the United States. We became good friends. I could write a chapter about this remarkable man. We discussed religions during a long drive we took together. He admitted that the Christian religion reached higher ideals than any other, but said that the experiment of practising Christianity had never been tried, and he thought that Confucianism actually practised was better than Christianity without a trial. He compared our military preparations and battleships with the Chinese idea of building an expensive wall between China and its enemies. Christians he said, wanted to kill enemies while Confucius counselled protection against them. He professed to believe that if Christ made a tour through China He would pronounce the Chinese as living more in accordance with His teachings than the America which professed to be following Him.

McKinley was elected in November, 1896, and announced himself during an address before the National Association of Manufacturers in New York, as a gold-standard advocate. I heard this address and congratulated him. The President and I, by the way, became good friends. In a talk I had with him in Washington he told me that he admitted he had been a little extreme in his tariff views, while he thought I had gone a little too far the other way. He said we ought to meet on a common ground, adding that he expected to make an address shortly in Buffalo that he thought would please me. He agreed with Blaine as to the policy of reciprocity. This was some time after the period about which we are now writing—in other words, not long before his assassination in Buffalo. McKinley was a very lovable character, and was one of our best-loved presidents. His devotion to his wife and his kindly disposition made an appeal everywhere.

Early in 1898 the *Maine* arrived in the harbour of Havana on a friendly mission, and shortly afterward was destroyed—I have always supposed by an internal explosion. There has never been the slightest proof that the Spanish Government or any Spanish official had anything to do with destroying this vessel, and it is hardly credible that Spain should do such an insane thing as to provoke a war with the United States. I have already mentioned an interview which some senators had with President Cleveland with regard to war with Spain which Congress was inclined to declare, and am glad to say that in a talk with President McKinley he agreed with Cleveland. But after the destruction of the *Maine* nothing could stop a war. The declaration of war against Spain of course seriously disturbed business for a time; indeed from the beginning of 1893 to the close of 1898 business was not in a very satisfactory condition. Our country gained great credit by the terms of the treaty giving Cuba complete independence, with the wise provision of the Platt Amendment. Senator Orville Platt, by the way, was one of our ablest senators, and well known to me.

I have had many dealings with what might be called professional politicians. Some of them have had principles and have been in politics because they liked public life. Some men have a perfectly legitimate liking for political office and they usually make the best public servants. Some men go into public life for what they can get out of it in a money way, but I have a feeling, drawn from experience, that it is never the money that most counts. I have been with politicians who had principles and with some who had none. But I have found any and every kind of politician as a rule more effective than the reformers. For the politicians usually manifest common sense in which the reformers are often lacking.

In June, 1900, William McKinley was renominated for President for a second term and Theodore Roosevelt for Vice-President. The politicians of New York were very uneasy over Roosevelt's growing popularity and wished to bury him in the vice-presidency. I was in Philadelphia during the Convention. Mr. Roosevelt did not want the nomination. He protested against it, but the enthusiasm for him was even greater than that for the presidential candidate, and he was simply borne away by the tide and forced to accept.

This was my first acquaintance with the great personality of Theodore Roosevelt, and my admiration for him grew every time I saw him. McKinley was elected by a great majority, a large portion of which was due to the popularity of the vice-presidential candidate.

I had frequent contacts with this most admirable American. Through Jacob Riis I knew a great deal about him when he was Police Commissioner of New York, for I have always been a student of criminology and penology—more particularly of penology.

In May, 1902, we had the great anthracite coal strike in Pennsylvania, with great suffering and disturbance of business interests generally. This strike was settled by President Roosevelt. He called a meeting of the mine owners and told them that they must go back and mine coal. President Baer of the Reading Coal Co. gave me a graphic account of this interview. He said:

"I took one look at Roosevelt's face and made up my mind we should have to go back and mine coal."

They did, making a satisfactory arrangement with the workmen who had already been interviewed by the President's agent, and were in the mood for compromise.

In June, 1914, I went to Europe in a semi-public capacity as a member of the Southern Commercial Congress, under instructions of the Secretary of State, to look into conditions of municipalities with a view to adopting some of their best practices here. I landed at Hamburg in July, travelled through Germany two or three weeks before the outbreak of the Great War and talked with bankers and business men. I did not meet a single one who had a word to say about war or had any idea, apparently, that the world's greatest catastrophe was so near at hand. A knowledge of the coming war and the plans for it seem to have been entirely confined to the Kaiser and his military clique.

I went on out to Bulgaria and reaching there presented my credentials at the Palace and was entertained by the King and Queen. Queen Eléonora was a beautiful character. I went with her to her charitable institutions and talked with her over her plans for the progress of their country. The King was very much interested in forestry. We had a congenial subject there. His botanical garden was exceedingly attractive. They spoke English with scarcely an accent; indeed the King and Queen spoke several languages. My interpreter who went with me spoke thirteen languages. I told him that any one who could speak Bulgarian should naturally be able to talk in any other language.

Part of the object which took me to Europe was to look into our interests there. We had business in Bulgaria and had sold quite a number of engines, boilers, and threshers, and I was naturally interested in looking into conditions. The declaration of war with Serbia alarmed me, and I began to make arrangements to return. Before I left Bulgaria, however, war had been declared by Russia, France, and England. I found the railroad had stopped running, but I determined to return if possible by way of Constantinople. When I finally reached that city, I found everything in wild commotion, banks closed, hotels requiring bills to be paid in advance, no letters of credit honoured, and orders given that no gold should be paid out. Our ambassador, Mr. Morgenthau, was very gracious to me. He entertained me at his house up the Bosphorus and in his residence in Constantinople, a very creditable place, by the way—I believe one of the only two creditable embassies owned by our Government—the other being at Yokohama. The Dardanelles, however, were mined and transportation was dead. A few freight vessels were permitted to pass through at their own risk. I succeeded in getting away on a freight vessel, expecting to land at Athens and cross over to Brindisi in Italy, but found they were mobilizing in Athens and transportation had stopped. Our freight vessel continued on its course and finally landed me at Syracuse, and from there I went by rail to Rome. I finally got passage on the *San Guglielmo*, an emigrant ship from Naples, with a number of other Americans. I could make quite a story of my experiences. I reached home safely the last of August and found the factory running on part time, the business conditions reminding me of the conditions during '73. My trunk was lost in Europe but it came through finally in February, 1921, seven years afterward, with nothing disturbed.

*   *   *   *   *

And now, in conclusion, what does it all mean? What have these years taught me? Nothing of a startling nature—the incidents fade—but these principles remain:

(1) That it is, as a rule, safe to trust human beings. Comparatively few are unfair, if you are fair yourself.

(2) That troubles and apparent difficulties are but stepping-stones to progress—the most practical way of learning—and, as Greeley said, "The way to resume is to resume."

(3) That there is nothing that will take the place of work, either to gain success or to gain happiness or to gain both—and I think it is possible to gain both if, in the striving and working for success, the dollar is not put above the man.

(4) That one can and must keep faith with oneself.

(5) That God is not mocked. You cannot break his laws without suffering.

(6) That one's only dangerous enemy is oneself. In the ultimate no one can hurt you but yourself.

(7) That friends are among the greatest assets— and the way to get friends is to be a friend.

(8) That one should never seek anything for which one does not give value. This avoids the disposition to speculate—which is one of the greatest dangers that beset the business man.

Following these rules, the world grows in interest and life is happier with gathering years.

THE END

INDEX

INDEX

CPSIA information can be obtained at www.ICGtesting.com
Printed in the USA
LVOW03s1810250914

405886LV00012B/343/P